The Folklore of The British Isles
General Editor : Venetia J. Newall

The Folklore
of Sussex

D0713272

The Folklore of Sussex

Jacqueline Simpson

Drawings by Gay John Galsworthy

B. T. BATSFORD LTD LONDON

'In memory of my father'

First published 1973
© Jacqueline Simpson 1973

0 7134 0240 7

Printed in Great Britain by
Bristol Typesetting Co. Ltd. Bristol
for the Publishers
B. T. Batsford Ltd 4 Fitzhardinge Street London W1H 0AH

Foreword

In his monumental work *The British Folklorists* (London, 1968), Professor Richard M. Dorson sadly refers to the ' fading of the British folklore movement' at the time of the First World War. Later he pays tribute to the work of Katharine Briggs, Iona and Peter Opie, and one or two other scholars. Granting that there is substance in his basic view, it might now seem more appropriate to have used the term ' temporary eclipse '.

Since his book was published we have seen the continued achievements of Katharine Briggs, and the Opies have added to their researches in the field of children's lore. Yet it is true that much remains to be done, and a public appeal on the day that I write this underlines the need for still greater efforts in recording the lore and games of schoolchildren. It is not necessary to confine such an appeal to the activities of the young since, in times of ever more efficient and all-pervading mass communications, the fluidity of tradition is greatly intensified. This appeal drew particular attention to the influence of television and advertising jingles, but there is no need to stress the effect of numerous modern pressures on tradition as a whole. This is not to say that folklore and custom disappear: rather that the new or the variant is superimposed on the old with increased rapidity.

This volume by Jacqueline Simpson is therefore especially welcome, not only because of its wide scope, which can be seen from a glance through her own Introduction, but also because, for the first time, it brings together in an easily accessible form the folklore of Sussex. She has assembled material not hitherto published, or drawn from widely scattered sources, and presented it in such a way as to stimulate interest and collection in her own County and elsewhere. This, as I have stressed, is essential and her volume is prepared in a manner calculated to entrance and arouse the enthusiasm of the general reader and the scholar. Both have their part to play.

Jacqueline Simpson's own scholarship is already well known to those familiar with her other work, notably the *Penguin English Dictionary* and her attractive and readable presentation of Icelandic folktales. She combines a delightful style and charming wit with meticulous scholarship and the present volume is a fitting compliment to her accomplishments in other fields. She has for many years been a member of the Folklore Society's Committee and her interesting and incisive contributions to the Society's Journal are much appreciated by members. It is therefore a particular pleasure to me to welcome this brilliant young scholar as the first contributor to what it is hoped will be built into a comprehensive series on the folklore of the British Isles.

London University
February 1973   Venetia Newall

Contents

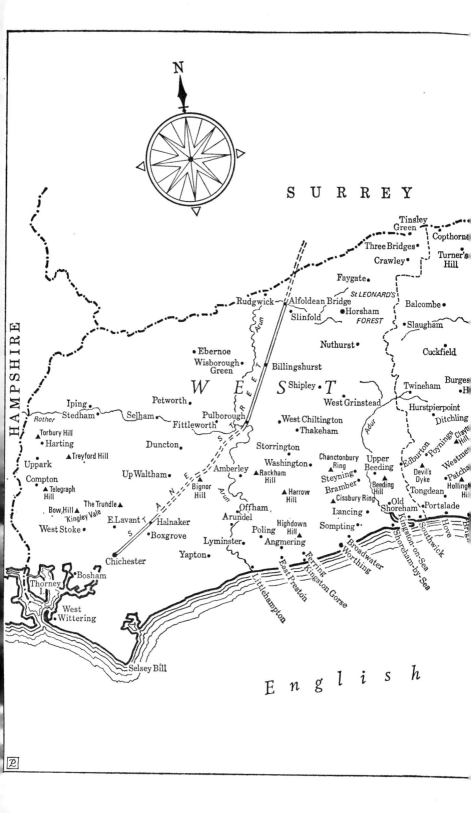

SUSSEX

KENT

t Grinstead
Hartfield •   • Withyham

ASHDOWN   Crowborough
FOREST   • Rotherfield   Ticehurst •
ted   • Duddleswell   Mayfield   *Rother*   Etchingham •   Bodiam   Playden
nes   • Burwash   Rye
         E   A   S   T   Udimore
    • Fletching   • Brightling   Brede •   Winchelsea
    Uckfield •   Heathfield •   • Netherfield
Ouse   Warbleton •   • Battle
    Isfield •   Halland   • Fairlight
Barcombe   Chiddingly •   *Cuckmere*   Hurstmonceux •   • Ninfield   Hollington
ton   • Hellingly   • Hooe   *Bulverhythe* *Hastings*
g ▲Mt   • Ringmer   • Hailsham
n   Harry   • Lewes   • Arlington   *Pevensey*
er Mt ▲   Glynde
    Caburn Selmeston •   • Wilmington
Kingston-   Firle ▲ • Burlow Castle
nr-Lewes   Beacon
Piddinghoe • Berwick • Windover Hill
           Alfriston • Litlington
Rottingdean Hindover ▲   East Dean   *Eastbourne*
           Hill
           Newhaven *Seaford*

C   h   a   n   n   e   l

0 1 2 3 4 5   10   15
                                  miles

Acknowledgments

Thanks are due to the following authors and publishers for permission to quote from the books and journals mentioned (page references are to *The Folklore of Sussex*): Bob Copper *A Song for Every Season*, Wm Heinemann Ltd (1971) for pages 114–15, 121 and 127–8; A. Beckett *The Wonderful Weald*, Mills & Boon Ltd (1911) for pages 157–8; L. Grant *A Chronicle of Rye*, Noel Douglas (1927) for page 39; *Folklore* (LXIX, 1958) for page 93; W. D. Parish *A Dictionary of Sussex Dialect* (revised by Helena Hall), Gardners, Bexhill (1957) for page 38; *Sussex County Magazine* for pages 41–2, 52, 58–9, 70–2, 74, 77–8, 85, 105–6 and 138; *West Sussex Gazette* for pages 23–4, 103–4, 110, 139–40 and 149; M. Wright *Cuckfield, an Old Sussex Town*, C. Clarke, Haywards Heath (1971) for pages 48–9; M. Wyndham *Mrs Paddick*, Chapman & Hall Ltd (1947) for pages 105 and 107.

Introduction

THERE HAVE BEEN MANY BOOKS written about Sussex, its history and the beauties of its countryside, but in all of them its folklore, legends and folk-customs receive only minor and incidental mention, or, at the best, a single chapter. Yet the foundations for the study of Sussex lore had been well laid in the nineteenth century by three pioneers whose essays, though brief, are crammed with valuable material – M. A. Lower, who recorded several local legends (two of them verbatim) in his *Contributions to Literature* (1854) and in an article in *Sussex Archaeological Collections* XIII (1861); Mrs Charlotte Latham, who published a collection of 'West Sussex Superstitions' in *Folk-Lore Record* I (1878); and F. E. Sawyer, who listed many seasonal customs in *Sussex Archaeological Collections* XXXIII (1883), and also produced a pamphlet on *Sussex Place-Rhymes and Local Proverbs* (1884).

This promising beginning, however, was never systematically followed up, though many individual items appeared in various scattered sources. Local historians describing their own towns and villages would often include two or three local tales and super-stitions, while some of the more colourful legends attached to topographical features naturally appear again and again in general descriptions of the county. First-hand accounts of customs and festivals are also found in the reminiscences of people who have known rural working-class life from the inside, notably Harry Burstow in 1911 and Bob Copper in 1971, but books of this type are unfortunately rare. The *Sussex County Magazine* (1926–56) includes a good many articles and letters touching on points of folklore; many are of great value, being based on first-hand observation or personal memories, but a few merely repeat, with-out acknowledgement, material drawn from older printed sources. Of particular interest are the articles contributed by Miss L. N. Candlin to the *Sussex County Magazine* and to the *West Sussex Gazette* over the last thirty years or so, since these are drawn from her own family traditions (particularly concerning the Washington, Brighton and Lewes areas), and from oral informants in many parts of Sussex. I am very grateful to her for allowing me the free use of this material, and for supplementing it with further information in conversation and correspondence.

The aim of the present book, therefore, is to give a coherent picture of the considerable amount of Sussex folklore which has been recorded over the last hundred years or more, and some of which is still very much alive today. Broadly speaking, the material falls into four main categories. First, local legends; that is to say, stories that are attached to some particular place (whether it be to a natural feature such as a wood or pool, to a visible archaeological feature such as a burial mound, or to a church, house or monument), or else to some particular person whose notoriety or eccentricity serves to attract anecdotes. The actual content of such legends is very often supernatural, fantastic or grotesque; they include tales of buried treasures, lost bells, giants, bogeymen, dragons, fairies, ghosts, witches, and the Devil. Occasionally they are not merely linked to well-known landmarks, but are vouched for by their narrators as having happened to 'a man my great-grandfather knew', or perhaps even to a closer friend or relative. Such stories have a good chance of surviving well in oral tradition, since once one has heard the legend attached to a prominent building or landmark, it is almost impossible to see the place without remembering the story.

The second major category is that of traditional beliefs and magical practices. Two chapters are devoted to particular aspects of this field – non-rational healing methods, and beliefs concerned with the human life-cycle – while others are mentioned in the chapters about the Devil, fairies, and witches. Thirdly comes the very extensive category of seasonal observances; this includes a varied assortment of festivals, ceremonies, customs, games, rituals, beliefs and sayings which are linked to particular dates. Here the main emphasis is on what the community, or certain groups within it, actually do in obedience to tradition, rather than on their stories and beliefs. Needless to say, there is no town or village that ever observed every single one of the seasonal customs; I have been careful to name precise localities wherever possible. Finally, there are the stock rhymes, sayings and anecdotes applied to inhabitants of certain villages by their neighbours. Sussex people have not been saddled with a regional 'character' to the same extent as, say, Scotsmen and Yorkshiremen; on a more local level, however, taunts and teasing sayings are quite plentiful.

Local legends, as has been remarked already, are closely linked to topographical features, especially those which seem in any way mysterious. They may be dramatic natural formations, such as prominent hills and steep coombes ascribed to the Devil's work, or to a giant (pp 29, 62–3), or man-made structures whose age and purpose had been forgotten. It is noteworthy that all the hills alleged to have treasure buried on them are the sites of Iron Age forts (pp 23–5), that several spots named as fairy haunts are prehistoric or medieval earthworks (pp 53, 58), and that certain barrows are associated with the Devil or with giants (pp 28–30, 61). Other conspicuous archaeological features mentioned in legends are the Long Man of Wilmington and Stane Street (pp 27–9, 61).

There is an obvious connexion between coastal erosion and legends of lost churches (pp 21–2), while particularly deep places in rivers, bogs, moats and harbours have attracted stories of sunken bells (pp 20–3). In three of these the name 'Bell Hole' occurs, and the name may well have given rise to the legend rather than vice versa; it has been suggested that in these cases 'bell' is a corruption of the dialect word *pell*, which simply means a deep hole in a river. Then again there are the strange pools called Knucker Holes, sometimes said to have monsters in them, the outstanding example being at Lyminster (pp 38–42); dense isolated woods may be reputed haunted; oddly-placed or con-spicuous buildings, notably churches, have their typical stories too. Indeed, so close is the correlation between landscape and legend that it would hardly be an exaggeration to say that every landmark and almost every building mentioned in this book is notable in its own right, quite apart from the story attached to it.

History too is reflected in legends, albeit in a very simplified form, and often distorted by mistaken antiquarian theories which linger on at popular level long after they are discarded by scholars. Thus, it was once thought that the name Alfriston meant 'Alfred's Town', and this idea fostered the growth of legends that Alfred fought the Danes nearby, and even that an iron pot dis-played in the Star Inn was the very one in which he burned the cakes. Danes occur quite often in Sussex stories, even though the county suffered relatively little from their raids. One tale about them, concerning the battle in Kingley Vale (p 46), may well be based on fact; there are two others in which any original factual basis has vanished beneath fictional motifs (the raid on Bosham, pp 20–1, and an alleged battle which Alfred fought against them on Terrible Down near Isfield, in which men waded knee-deep in blood); and one which is a sheer fantasy inspired by place-names – that Danish warriors cut withies at Withy Pits near Three Bridges to conceal their numbers, but were turned back at Turner's Hill and crawled away to Crawley. Clearly, when folk-imagination functions in this way, it is rash to seek historical information from tales about colourful figures of the far past, such as Druids, Danes, or Julius Caesar. Oddly enough, the most momentous event that ever took place on Sussex soil, the Battle of Hastings, has left only minor traces on its tales (pp 19, 46–7).

Even stories about comparatively modern personages are often unreliable. Charles II figures in Sussex lore because he passed through the county when fleeing to France in 1651; oral tradition has so multiplied his alleged hiding-places and overnight stops on the journey that one wonders how he ever reached the coast at all. The famous episode of his hiding in an oak tree after the battle of Worcester has inspired Sussex imitations; he is said to have hidden in a yew near St Leonard's Forest, where 'an old woman came out and gave him some pease pudden', and also, more plausibly, in a hollow elm in what are now the grounds of the Royal Pavilion, Brighton. This latter tale has been handed down among the descendants of a Brighton boatman who sailed on the king's ship, yet even this excellent provenance cannot stifle an uneasy suspicion that there would have been no elm at Brighton if there had been no oak at Boscobel.

The broad trends of popular feeling have left more solid traces in folk tradition – such things as the anti-Catholic prejudice which accounted for the intensity of the Guy Fawkes celebrations at Lewes and elsewhere, and perhaps for some ogre legends too (see pp 31–3). This feeling, however, never suppressed the legends of local saints, nor could it entirely erase traces of old Catholic customs such as 'souling' (p 134), laying money on coffins (p 112), and possibly the form of wassailing described on p 145. And it is almost unnecessary to point out the close links between certain crafts and ways of life and particular stories and customs – blacksmiths had their craft legend and their feast of Old Clem (pp 138–40); cobblers their St Crispin feast (pp 131–3); shepherds their tall stories, tales of sheep-stealers, and beliefs about 'wish hounds' (pp 50, 157); carters their tales of carts bewitched (pp 70–2); bellringers their tales of lost bells (pp 22–3); while the connexion between agriculture and many seasonal customs is immediately obvious. The smugglers hold a particular place in folklore, for they are thought to have encouraged all sorts of supernatural beliefs and stories as a cover for their own activities; in addition, of course, their exploits are often locally remembered, their alleged tunnels are talked of to this day (pp 25–6), and their ghosts are often said to walk.

It must also be said that the stories collected in this book, though 'real Sussex' in the sense that they have been cherished here for several generations at least, cannot be considered exclusive to this county – on the contrary, very many can be matched in other parts of England. The story of the Hangman's Stone (p 157) is told also of rocks in Northumberland and on Exmoor; the stolen Bosham Bell has a counterpart at Whitby Abbey, Yorkshire; the story of the lost Slinfold Bell shares its white oxen and its verse with that of Great Tom of Kentsham; there are irremovable skulls like those of Warbleton Priory (pp 47–8) in various houses in Dorset, Yorkshire, Lancashire and Westmorland; the upside-down burial on Highdown Hill (p 45) can be matched on Box Hill, Surrey; the bogey called Spring-Heeled Jack (p 31) was feared by London children too – and these are but a few examples from what could be a long list. The same holds good for beliefs and for most seasonal customs too; they are traditional in Sussex, but not unique to her. Regional differences do exist in folklore, but they seldom follow county boundaries.

Inevitably the question arises, at what period did these tales, beliefs and customs flourish most? And how old are they? No general answer is possible; each case must be assessed on the evidence available, which all too often is less full than one would wish. I have given the oldest source known to me for each item in the notes at the end of the book, but in most cases it is obvious that the story or custom was already old by the time it was first mentioned in print. Roughly speaking, the picture given here refers primarily to the nineteenth century and the first few years of the twentieth, the period which was brought to a close by the First World War and by the revolution in modern agriculture and transport. When the tale or belief remained current in more recent times, I have indicated this.

But it would be wrong to assume that there is no folklore to be found nowadays; on the contrary, it is quite easy to find people, including young people in their teens and twenties, who know local traditions which have reached them orally, not from any printed source. It is indeed very likely that some Sussex readers of this book will be reminded of stories, beliefs or customs in their own districts which I have not mentioned, or of variant versions of the stories I do tell; information about such items would be most welcome.

Finally, I wish to express my thanks to the staff of the Reference Department in Worthing Public Library, who laid before me the rich resources of their Sussex Room; to Miss L. N. Candlin, whose valuable contribution has been mentioned already; to many friends in and around Worthing who (sometimes unwittingly) added items to the list; and to Mrs Venetia Newall for additional information and encouragement.

Worthing, 1972   JACQUELINE SIMPSON

1 Churches, Bells and Treasures

ONE WOULD EXPECT THAT CHURCHES, by virtue of their prominent place in the landscape and in village life, would be the subjects of many and various types of legend; in fact, however, stories about them are predominantly of one type only, the 'foundation legend' – that is, a tale which purports to explain some peculiarity in the siting or structure of the church.

One such is at Alfriston; it is a cruciform building dating from around 1360, and it stands at some little distance from the houses, on what is probably an ancient Saxon mound, on the Tye, the village green. The real reason for the choice of this site may very well have been its comparative safety from flooding in a rather low-lying area, but legend ascribes it to supernatural guidance. The foundations were first laid, so the story goes, in a field just west of the village street, but the work made no progress, since every morning the builders found that all the stones they had laid the previous

B

day had been uprooted, whirled through the air, and flung onto the mound on the Tye. They were puzzled and anxious, not knowing whether the supernatural force at work was a Heavenly one, to be obeyed, or diabolical, to be resisted. But after some days of this, a wise man noticed four oxen lying on the Tye with their rumps touching, so as to form an equal-armed Cross. The sacred sign formed by these innocent beasts was taken as settling the matter, and accordingly a church, cruciform in construction, was built upon the Tye.

There is a similar tale about Udimore Church, though here it is the name, rather than the site, which provoked the legend. It is said that the site originally chosen was on the opposite side of the river Ree to that on which the church stands now, but every night the stones were miraculously shifted across, while a voice was heard calling out: 'O'er the mere! O'er the mere!' Hence the present site was chosen, and hence the name of the village arose. The explanation of the name is not in fact correct (it actually comes from 'Uda's Mere'), but at any rate it becomes a trifle less implausible when one remembers that in broad Sussex dialect the sound 'th' becomes 'd'.

At Hollington, on the other hand, it was the Devil who was held responsible for the curious site of the church, on the outskirts of Hastings, quite a distance from any centre of population, and surrounded by thick woods. There are two slightly divergent accounts, both dating from the 1840s. Both start by telling how, when men of a nearby village tried to build a church, each day's work was undone during the night. According to the first, all the building materials used simply to vanish into thin air, and this continued until the day when 'a countryman, happening to pass through an unfrequented wood, found there, to his no small surprise, a church newly built; the Evil One having contrived, since he could not utterly prevent the erection, to get it placed where no one could easily approach it'.

According to the other account, the angry workmen resorted to exorcism when they found their work spoilt:

> Priests were summoned to lay the fiend, and they had prepared to commence their potent conjurements, when a voice was heard offering to desist from opposition if the building were erected on the spot which he should indicate. The offer was accepted. The church was raised, and then there sprung up

around it a thick wood, concealing it from the general gaze.

Yet another variant on this theme is the legend attached to Battle Abbey Church, built by William the Conqueror in thanksgiving for his victory. It is said that he dreamed that his descendants would rule England for as many years as the nave of the church he was planning would have feet in its length. He therefore ordered the foundations to be marked out at 500 feet, but every night they were miraculously cut back to 315 feet, till the proud king accepted the verdict of Heaven, and allowed building to proceed on this reduced scale. Actually, this legend is rather unsatisfactory, for the date it indicates, 1381, is not particularly significant in our dynastic history. Perhaps the story really belongs to some other church with different dimensions, and has only become transferred to Battle Abbey by accidental confusion.

The founding of a church may also be a major point in a saint's legend. Everyone who has visited Steyning probably knows how St Cuthman pushed his mother in a wheelbarrow from Devon to Sussex, waiting for some sign from Heaven to show him where he should settle and build a church. As he came into Steyning, the barrow broke, and he cut some withies from a hedge to make a rope to mend it. Haymakers working in Penfold Field (which is still also sometimes known as Cuthman's Field) burst out laughing at his stupidity. 'Laugh man, weep Heaven,' answered Cuthman, and at once a heavy cloudburst drenched that field, and that field only. And from that day to this, it always rains on that one meadow in haymaking time; indeed, some call it 'the Accursed Field', and declare that nothing will grow upon it. Meanwhile, St Cuthman had struggled a little further on his way, but again the barrow broke, this time beyond repair. Suddenly he realised that this was the sign he had been waiting for, and on this spot he later built the first church at Steyning, a timber one. It said that Christ Himself appeared in the guise of a travelling carpenter, and helped Cuthman to raise a roof-beam which was more than his own skill could manage.

A church may also become a bone of contention between a Saint and the Devil. It is said that Satan, furious at certain humiliating defeats he had suffered at the hands of St Dunstan (see pp 63–4) bided his time until the saint embarked on building a wooden church at Mayfield. Then he came in the night and gave the whole church such a thrust that it leaned all askew;

but next day St Dunstan, who was of more than human size and strength, set it upright again with a single heave of his shoulder. Once more, Satan waited for his revenge – indeed, having grown wiser, he waited until the saint was dead. Then, when men of a later generation wished to build a fine new stone church, he undid their day's work each night, and also pestered the stonemasons in their quarry, where the mark of his hoofs was long pointed out. How he was foiled the story does not say, but foiled he must have been, for Mayfield Church, dedicated to St Dunstan, now stands completed and in its rightful place.

If churches attract legends, so too do their bells. Indeed, bells hold a great fascination for the imagination, because of their holiness and beauty, their power against evil spirits, and the slightly eerie sense of mystery which surrounds them. Particularly memorable are the legends of lost church bells, and Sussex has its full share of these. The most famous, undoubtedly, is that of the Bosham bell, which first appeared in print in the late nineteenth century, but must certainly be far older. There are some variations of detail, but the main outline of the tale is this:

In the days of Alfred the Great, Bosham was a flourishing port, with a fine church and rich monastery; but in those days, also, the Sussex coast was frequently attacked by bands of Viking raiders. One day a Viking ship was sighted making for Bosham harbour, and at this not only the farmers and fishermen but even the priests and monks fled inland, taking with them whatever valuables they could carry away, and abandoning the rest of their goods to fate. So it happened that when the raiders landed they found the church undefended, and were able to carry off the great tenor bell, the finest in the whole peal. They lashed it to the cross-benches of their ship, and set sail, delighted with their prize.

Meanwhile, the monks crept back to their plundered church. When they saw the enemy making for the open sea, they rang the remaining bells – some say, in thanksgiving for their own safety, but some say, in a backwards peal, as a solemn curse on the sacrilegious Danes. The ship was nearing the mouth of the estuary when this peal came ringing across the water, and at the sound the stolen bell broke loose from its moorings and replied, in a single loud note; then it crashed through the ship's hull, so that bell and ship and men all vanished beneath the waves. There are some, however, who deny that the ship sank; they say its shattered planking closed again at once, and not one drop came in – a miracle which converted the heathen Danes on the spot. But all agree that the bell itself disappeared into the depths, at the spot which is now called Bosham Deep, but was formerly known as Bell Hole. And all agree that whenever the bells ring from Bosham Church, the sunken one still answers from beneath the waves.

Now the men of Bosham grieved for their lost bell, and many times they tried to recover it, but could never do so. At length, centuries after it had first been lost, a man who was knowledgeable about such matters told them that there was one way to raise it, but only one. They must find a team of pure white oxen (or, some say, white horses), harness them to the bell, and so draw it up on shore. The team was assembled, after much searching; a rope was fastened to the bell, and the oxen began to haul. All went well; the huge shape of the bell could be glimpsed as it was gradually drawn into shallow water; then all at once, when it had almost touched land, the rope snapped, and the bell rolled back into the depths – for, though nobody had noticed this, on one of the oxen there was a single black hair. So the Bosham Bell was lost again, this time for good, and only its answering note is ever heard.

It has more than once been suggested that the 'answer' is in fact an echo thrown back across the harbour from woods on the opposite shore, though I have not come on any first-hand account from anyone claiming to have heard such an echo himself. But the legend itself is locally very well known, and there is sometimes added to it a little rhyme, the call of the lost bell:

> Ye bells of Bosham, ring for me,
> For as ye ring, I ring wi' ye.

There are traditions too, though less widely known than this one, about the bells of churches that have been covered by the sea as a result of coastal erosion. At Bulverhythe, where much of the old village has been destroyed in this way, local fishermen say they 'can hear the bells of Bulverhythe' whenever the waves make a loud raking sound on the shingle, and that this means either bad weather or an approaching thaw. The saying was first recorded in 1884, and is still sometimes heard. Similarly, men who fished the shallow banks off Selsey Bill, where the old town of Selsey stood, used to believe that at very low tides they could sometimes hear the bells of the sunken cathedral of St Wilfred sounding underwater, out by the Owers Light. This tradition is remembered still, as are others of the same type about a lost village and its bell off Kingston Gorse, near Ferring, and off Pett Level, near Hastings.

Inland churches have their lost bells too. Near Isfield, at the junction of the Ouse and the Iron River, it is said that a bell was hurled into the river by over-zealous Puritans, at a spot called Bell Hole Brook; while at Etchingham, whose church was formerly surrounded by a moat, it is said that a bell lies hidden underground where the moat once was, and that it can never be raised again unless six white oxen drag it out. Both these legends were first mentioned in print in 1861, and are still current; similar tales were told of Hurstmonceux and Arlington, in the latter case associated with another 'Bell Hole', a deep pool in the Cuckmere River.

Very much alive, even now, is the tale of the Alfoldean Bell (also sometimes referred to as the Slinfold, Rudgwick, or Nowhurst Bell). Alfoldean is a bridge spanning the Arun about a mile and a half north of Slinfold, near the point where the old Roman road called Stane Street (now the A29 from Pulborough) joins the A281 from Horsham to Guildford; the spot is also known as Roman Gate. The ground thereabouts was, until recent times, very swampy.

There has long been a tradition in and around the villages of Slinfold and Rudgwick (traceable far back into the nineteenth century, and surely older still) that a bell was once lost in a bog at this spot. According to Harry Burstow, a Horsham bell-ringer who was born in 1826, this took place in the times of the Roman occupation – by which he may perhaps have meant the days when England was a Roman Catholic land. The bell, he said, had been cast in Rome itself, and was being taken up Stane Street from Chichester on its way to York, where it was to be hung in York Minster. But according to John Pullen, also a bell-ringer and a Rudgwick man, it was near the end of its journey, being destined for Rudgwick Church, only a few miles away. But both agree that it fell from the waggon and rolled into the swamp at Alfoldean, where it remains to this day, despite an attempt to raise it with a team of white oxen or heifers.

The story of this attempt is best told in the words of Stephen Peacock of Slinfold, who heard the tale from his father of the same name, who was born in 1829 and died in 1911; the elder Peacock had himself learnt the story from an old carter named

Pete Greenfield, who worked on Dedisham Manor Farm, the estate nearest to Alfoldean Bridge:

> They went to a cunning 'ooman [i.e. a white witch], and she told them that if they got twelve white oxen and went to the spot at midnight, they could raise the bell. But no one was to say a word, or speak. So, the story goes, one night they went with twelve white oxen which they hooked on to the bell in the bog. Then, just as the oxen drew the old bell to the top of the bog, one of the men shouted out:

> We've got the Alfoldean gurt bell,
> In spite of all the devils in hell!

> At that moment the chain which held it broke, the bell slipped back, and they never got it after all.

So strong is this tradition, and so precise the information it gives as to the site of the lost bell, that in 1971 a dowser was called in to locate it; his report was encouraging, and an excavation was carried out at the spot he indicated, but nothing was found.

I do not know whether dowsers have ever tried their skills at finding the various traditional treasures allegedly buried on the Sussex Downs, but if they should wish to, there is no lack of such sites – all prominent hills, and, in almost every case, crowned with Iron Age forts. Such earthworks are mysterious enough in themselves to attract stories, and the excavations of archaeologists, the purpose of which certainly puzzled some local people considerably, must have reinforced the existing traditions.

The best best known and most detailed tradition is that of the Golden Calf on the Trundle, near Goodwood. The first allusion to it that I know of is in Brewer's *Dictionary of Phrase and Fable*, 1870, which merely states that 'Aaron's Golden Calf is buried in Rook's Hill' – this being the name of the hill as a whole, while the Trundle, strictly speaking, is the hill-fort on the summit. More detailed is a dialogue quoted in Parish's *Dictionary of Sussex Dialect*, 1875, to illustrate the countryman's conscientious avoidance of the Devil's name by a pointed use of the word 'he'; Parish does not name the hill in question, but it is generally assumed that he was referring to the Trundle:

'In the Down there's a golden calf buried; people know very well where it it is – I could show you any day.'
'Then why don't you dig it up?'
'Oh, it's not allowed; *he* wouldn't let them.'
'Has anyone ever tried?'
'Oh yes, but it's never there when you look; *he* moves it away.

E. C. Curwen, excavating the Trundle in 1928, found that the legend 'was much upon the lips of the people of Singleton during the progress of our excavation'. More recently still, a writer in the *West Sussex Gazette* gave more details of the sort of experience which, so the story goes, may be expected by those who try to unearth the treasure:

You know, there's many a one that tried . . . My Dad used to say as his grandfather got up early on Holy Sunday [i.e. Easter Sunday] an' went along to the place an' started digging. An' he actually ketched sight of a lump o' gold, an' then he was almost deafed by a clap o' thunder, an' when he looked again, the gold was gone.

There is also a quite different account of the treasure hidden on the Trundle, according to which it is not Aaron's calf at all, but a mass of gold and other booty gathered by a Viking host – the same vikings, indeed, who are said to have been slaughtered in Kingley Vale by men from Chichester (see below, p 46). Before setting out for this battle, they hid their hoard somewhere on the hill, and set a ghostly calf to guard it; on certain nights this calf may still be heard bleating, as it roams the wooded slopes below the Trundle.

The remaining Sussex treasure-legends are mostly bare statements of belief, without narrative detail. Thus, the Golden Calf is also said to lie on Clayton Hill (where there are barrows, though no fort), and to be protected by the Devil, in the same way as on the Trundle. Chanctonbury, Hollingbury, and Pulborough Mount conceal some unspecified treasure; on Mount Caburn there is a silver coffin and also (separately) a knight in golden armour; on Firle Beacon, a silver coffin; under the Long Man of Wilmington, 'one of the Romans in a gold coffin'.

Cissbury was the scene of a slightly more elaborate story, current in the 1860s. It was said that a blocked-up tunnel ran underground from Offington Hall to Cissbury Ring (a good two miles), and that at the far end of the tunnel there lay a treasure. The owner of the Hall 'had offered half the money to anyone who would clear out the subterranean passage, and several persons had begun digging, but had all been driven back by large snakes springing at them with open mouths and angry hisses'. The alleged existence of the tunnel is still remembered in Worthing, though Offington Hall has been demolished; the treasure and its guardian snakes, however, seem now to be forgotten.

The last of these hill-top legends concerns Torbery or Tarberry Hill, near South Harting. Though the nature of the treasure is not specified, it is reputed to be so splendid that a local rhyme declares:

> Who knows what Tarberry would bear
> Would plough it with a golden share.

Such, at least, was the version of the rhyme recorded in 1877. A more recent version somewhat ironically makes the use of a golden ploughshare a necessary condition, without which the gold cannot be unearthed – no doubt, on the principle that it takes money to make money:

> He who would find what Torbery would bear
> Must plough it with a golden share.

Finally, a treasure story attached to an old house, Chiddingly Place. In the main gallery of this Tudor mansion, there was, once upon a time, a crock of gold, over which brooded an evil spirit in the shape of a black hen. There she sat, night and day, never moving and never taking food, until one day a robber rashly tried to seize the gold. At this, the hen hurled herself at him with such violence that he fell senseless, and then flew away through the east window of the hall, bending two thick iron bars as she forced her way between them. They were pointed out long afterwards in proof of the tale. As for the fool-hardy thief, when he came round from his stunned condition, he was found to have gone mad, and he had to be rocked in a cradle for the rest of his days.

Before leaving the subject of buried treasures, it may be as well to say something about alleged underground passages, like the one mentioned above as running from Offington Hall to

Cissbury. There are great numbers of these, so many that it would be impossible to list them; typically, they are said to run from some conspicuous or ancient house to the nearest church, from a church or a house to the sea, or from a tower, obelisk or other 'folly'. The situation is confused by the occasional discovery of real short tunnels, or at any rate recesses, leading from old cellars and crypts, which may possibly have been once used as smugglers' hides. But the great majority of the legendary tunnels are quite impossibly long, and they can only be fictitious.

They seem to have a strong hold on the popular imagination, even nowadays, but oddly enough there are few interesting explanations attached to them, and nothing that can reasonably be called a story. The commonest reason given for their existence is that they were made as escape routes by smugglers; it may well be that smugglers encouraged people to believe in such tunnels, if only to distract attention from their real routes. They may also be said to be the work of monks, of Catholic priests hiding from persecution, or (in one case, that of Dedisham Manor) of King John seeking a ready escape from the barons! In Brighton, for obvious reasons, there is said to be one leading from the Pavilion to Mrs Fitzherbert's house. But on the whole, underground passages are a disappointment to the folklore collector, their dramatic possibilities having remained quite undeveloped.

2 Giants & Bogeymen

THE TALLEST MAN IN ENGLAND is a Sussex man – the famous Long Man of Wilmington, a gigantic figure, 226 feet long, cut in the turf on the steep northern flank of Windover Hill, facing Wilmington Priory. Nowadays his outline is permanently picked out in white bricks, and has been so since 1874; originally his form would have been simply 'drawn' by cutting away the turf from the white chalk, but in the course of time he had been allowed to become so overgrown as to be only dimly visible when the light fell obliquely or when snow lay longer in his outline, and so a restoration became essential. In his overgrown state, he was also sometimes locally known as the Green Man, but that name is now forgotten.

The age of such chalk-cut figures has been much debated; the Long Man has been ascribed to pretty well every period from the Neolithic to the late medieval, but nowadays it would be fairly generally conceded that the only realistic choice lies between the Celtic and the pre-Christian Anglo-Saxon periods. A recent theory plausibly compares his pose, as he stands with a staff in either hand, with that of a naked warrior in a horned helmet, carrying two spears, engraved on a belt-buckle found in a seventh-century Saxon grave at Finglesham, Kent. This figure, and others like it on Scandinavian helmets, are connected with the cult of a war-god, and may represent either the supernatural being or his human devotees. But, of course, staffs are not spears, and the Long Man wears no helmet. Presumably what happened was that when Sussex became Christian the distinctive emblems of the warrior god were deliberately turfed over, leaving an inoffensive giant, less objectionable to Christian eyes.

The giant must have remained locally popular, for only repeated scraping away the turf could have kept him in existence through the centuries so that he survived, however dimly, until he was given his permanent outline in late Victorian times. Scouring such a large figure must have been a considerable task, and it is probably fair to assume that it was a communal undertaking, enlivened by sports and merrymaking (as at the famous scourings of the White Horse of Uffington, in Berkshire), but unfortunately no records of such activity have survived.

Naturally, a local legend grew up to explain how such a figure was there at all. According to this, a living giant had once had his home on Windover Hill, but had been killed, and the figure was either a memorial to him or the actual outline of his body, drawn round him as he lay dead on the slope. As for how he died, the versions differ. Some say he simply tripped on the crest of the hill, which is very steep, and broke his neck; others, that he was killed by pilgrims on their way to Wilmington Priory (an echo, perhaps, of religious objections to, or mutilations of, the figure?); others, that he was killed by a shepherd who threw his dinner at him. But the commonest tale was that there were two giants, the one on Windover Hill, and the other living in the large round barrow on top of Firle Beacon, three miles away across the Cuckmere Valley. The two of them quarrelled, and hurled boulders at one another – some flint mines and quarries on Windover Hill are said to be the craters left by these missiles. At length, the Firle Giant killed the Long Man, either with a boulder or by flinging his hammer at him, and he now lies dead on the hillside – or else, say some, in a long barrow called Hunter's Burgh up on the crest of the hill.

One intriguing question that must tantalise both archaeologist and folklorist is whether the Sussex Downs, which lend themselves so well to the cutting of chalk figures, ever had any more of them besides the Long Man (apart, that is, from a horse on Hindover Hill, south of Alfriston, known to have been first cut about 1838 by some young men from Frog Firle, and re-cut in 1924). There are strong hints that older figures did once exist in this same region of the Cuckmere Valley. The late T. C. Lethbridge remembered being told by a shepherd, when he was a schoolboy at Seaford, that the Long Man had once had a companion, and that these figures had been known as Adam and Eve. Moreover, J. P. Emslie, collecting traditions in this area in 1905, came upon memories of a figure representing 'a man thrown from a horse' on a hill above Alfriston, which was locally said to mark the site of a victory of Saxons over Normans. Two other writers specifically locate a figure (possibly the same one) as having been on the slopes of Hindover Hill, a mile and a half south of Alfriston; one, A. H. Allcroft, says of it: 'Men who were schoolboys in the 1860s recollect it well enough, though it is now so vanished that learned folks refuse to believe them.'

To return to legends, rather than figures, there seems to have been a traditional Downland giant named Gill, for on the slopes of Mount Caburn, not far from Glynde, is a barrow known as Gill's Grave; at one time there was a story current that Gill used to stand on top of the Caburn and hurl his hammer from that height – though at whom is not said. Two other place names, Gill's Ridge near Crowborough and Gill's Lap in Ashdown Forest, may possibly allude to the same gigantic hero (though the latter is usually 'explained' by a rather pointless anecdote about a carter named Gill whose overlapping load upset his cart). There was also an unnamed giant in the neighbourhood of Lewes, who, so local children believed in the 1880s, had hollowed out the great coombe in the Downs behind the town.

The only giant associated with West Sussex is a more literary figure, Bevis of Hampton, the hero of a lengthy poem of the fourteenth century, who accomplished many exploits with the help of his horse Arundel (or Hirondelle) and his sword Morglay. The 'Hampton' of the poem is Southampton, but in Sussex lore Bevis, presumably because of his horse's name, is associated with the town of Arundel. He is here said to have been a giant, who could wade across from the Isle of Wight, and frequently did so, for his own amusement. He acted as warder at the gates of the Earls of Arundel, who built a tower to house him, and allowed him a whole ox and two hogsheads of beer each week. He served them loyally for many years, and when he grew old and felt that his end was near, he flung his sword from the top of the castle keep, and asked to be buried where it fell. A prehistoric burial mound in Arundel Park is known as Bevis's Grave, a huge sword in the armoury is alleged to be Morglay, and the tower called Bevis Tower is pointed out as his home.

Bosham too has a legend about Bevis. He is said to have been in the habit of pausing there to wash his dogs when on his way from Southampton to Arundel, on which occasions he generally had with him a staff which he used to use when he went wading across from the Isle of Wight. This staff he eventually gave to Bosham Church as a keepsake – and to prove the tale, people used at one time to point to a large pole kept in the church tower, though by the end of the nineteenth century it had been removed. A few miles inland from Bosham, on Telegraph Hill near Compton, there is a fine prehistoric long barrow known as Bevis's Thumb.

The giants considered so far have been an amiable company, keeping their aggressiveness for one another, not for men. Very different are the bogeymen, terrifying figures whom children believed in, and whom parents deliberately used in order to scare their offspring into good behaviour. These bogeys might be, in origin, real human beings, but to the children they would easily seem supernatural in their ubiquity and omniscience; people still living can remember the nursery threat 'Boney will come and take you away,' which originated in the fear of the Napoleonic invasion, but continued long after Napoleon was no more. More ancient, and all the more fearsome for that, were the foes whom certain nineteenth-century mothers would invoke to control their children: 'I'll set the Danes on to yer, if yer doänt do as I tells yer!'

Some bogeys were only mentioned in connexion with a specific type of naughtiness; thus, 'if you go gathering firewood on Sunday, the Man in the Moon will carry you off', while 'if you go nutting on Sunday, the Devil will come and hold the branches down for you'. The point of both prohibitions, in this context, was to stop children spoiling their best clothes by rough use, but the one about nutting could have other meanings too (see pp 65–6).

One very impressive bogey was Spring-Heeled Jack. According to Miss Helena Hall's enlarged version of Parish's *Dictionary of*

Sussex Dialect, he was a real person, an early nineteenth-century practical joker who enjoyed alarming people walking by suddenly springing out at them. But to the children of Lewes in the 1890s he was a terrifying supernatural figure, extremely tall, and with such powerful springs in his heels that he could leap and rattle over hedges and ditches. Naughty children were told that he could spring so high that if they were not good he would peer in through their bedroom windows. Two Lewes boys were once thrown into utter panic by a glimpse of something white moving behind a hedge, with moaning sounds and clanking chains. They fled home, convinced that Spring-Heeled Jack was after them, but when their fathers went to investigate, the bogey proved to be a sick cow tethered in a field.

One odd and macabre type of legend, peculiar to East Sussex, alleges that some member of a prominent local family was an ogre who devoured babies. The Devenishes of Horselungs Manor, at Hellingly, and the Darrells of Scotney Castle (on the Kentish/ Sussex border) have each had this legend attached to one of their family, and the prominent Cavalier, Colonel Thomas Lunsford of Whyly, who was the target of several political satires, was accused in his own lifetime of this crime. One poem declares (inaccurately) that he was killed at the battle of Edgehill, and that there was a child's arm in his pocket at the time; another says that he fed his dogs on the scraps of his ghoulish meals; while in Butler's *Hudibras* he is jokingly compared with Bloody Bones, a traditional ogre in nursery lore. Finally, one may mention that four carved figures on the doorways of the seventeenth-century Socknersh Manor at Brightling are locally known as 'the Baby Eaters', though who they are meant to represent has been forgotten.

Such tales are grim enough, but the legend that has gathered round Sir Goddard Oxenbridge of Brede is more gruesome still, and has been elaborated over the centuries into a very satisfying tale of the macabre. Sir Goddard, who died in 1537, and whose monument can be seen in Brede Church, seems in fact to have been a quite normal and amiable person, piously concerned with endowing a chantry for the repose of his soul. In local legend, however, he has been transformed into a fearsome giant who roamed the countryside, carrying children off to eat them. Nobody could get at him to kill him, partly because of his great strength, and partly because a crow which was his familiar always brought him warning. Moreover, he was proof against all normal weapons, though it had been foretold that a wooden saw would be his death. Meanwhile, he was still unharmed, and every day he ate one child for his supper.

So at length, all the children of Sussex gathered together, and in great secrecy they brewed an enormous vat of beer (a drink previously unknown in the district), and fashioned a huge wooden saw. They brought the vat to Groaning Bridge, at the entrance to Brede Park, where Sir Goddard could not fail to see it, and they lay in ambush near the bridge. Sure enough, the giant saw the beer, smelled it, and began to drink; in next to no time he had drained the vat, and was lying helplessly drunk on the bridge. Then the children brought out their saw and laid it across him, as if across a fallen tree. Those from East Sussex rode upon one end of it, and those from West Sussex upon the other, and so they sawed Sir Goddard Oxenbridge in half. Long afterwards his ghost was still said to haunt both the house and the bridge, in the form of a severed trunk.

The status and origins of these grotesque tales of cannibalism are hard to determine – were they seriously believed, and if so, by whom, and why? It has been suggested by one Sussex historian, Edward Shoosmith, that they began as a local joke based on the existence of some article of food (e.g. a biscuit or pudding) familiarly known as a 'baby', but he was not able to offer evidence that any such food existed. On the other hand, the four reputed ogres do at least have one trait in common, namely their religious affiliations. Sir Goddard Oxenbridge and the Devenish family at Horselungs were Roman Catholics of the Reformation period, the Darrells of Scotney (including the 'Wild Darrell' to whom the legend is attached) remained recusant Catholics for several generations, and since Thomas Lunsford was a Cavalier leader, he must have been a High Church man. But Sussex on the whole sympathised with the Puritan and Parliamentarian movements, and honoured the memory of Protestant martyrs burned at Lewes in the reign of Mary Tudor.

I would hazard the guess that these legends reflect the deep religious and political hatreds of the sixteenth and seventeenth centuries, while that about Lunsford is (as indeed the contemporary literary allusions show) a deliberate atrocity story, circulated as war propaganda. Three of the stories were almost forgotten once the passions of the period died away, but that concerning Sir Goddard Oxenbridge was probably built up again by the eighteenth-century smugglers who are known to have used Brede Place as a hiding place, and so entered on a new lease of life; as late as 1947, there were still some who believed the house to be haunted by his grisly ghost.

3 Dragons of Land and Water

ALTHOUGH ST LEONARD cannot be truly claimed as a Sussex saint (he was a French hermit of the sixth century, later often revered by returning Crusaders who believed in his power to save them from captivity), a very long-standing legend asserts that he did actually live for many years in St Leonard's Forest, near Horsham, and moreover that he once killed a dragon there. The battle was long and ferocious, and as a reward for Leonard's courage, Heaven granted that wild lilies of the valley would spring up for ever wherever his blood had sprinkled the earth, and that nightingales which had previously distracted him by their singing while he was at prayer would henceforth be silent. Probably, too, it was once thought that the Forest would be rid of snakes for ever, since a traditional rhyme, probably dating from Tudor times, says of the Forest:

> Here the adders never sting,
> Nor the nightingales sing.

But the area certainly did not remain free from snakes. On the contrary, some very remarkable reptile was apparently repeatedly sighted in the Forest in 1614, and was circumstantially described in the following brief pamphlet (now in the Harleian Miscellany):

A True and Wonderful Discourse relating a strange and monstrous Serpent (or Dragon) lately discovered, and yet living, to the great Annoyance and divers Slaughters of both Men and Cattell, by his strong and violent Poison: in Sussex, two Miles from Horsam, in a Woode called St Leonard's Forrest, and thirtie Miles from London, this present Month of August, 1614. With the true Generation of Serpents.

In Sussex, there is a pretty market-towne, called Horsam, and neare unto it a forrest, called St Leonard's Forrest, and there is an unfrequented place, heathie, vaultie, full of unwholesome shades, and overgrowne hollowes, where this serpent is thought to be bred; but, wheresoever bred, certaine and too true it is, that there it yet lives. Within three or four miles compasse are its usual haunts, oftentimes at a place called Faygate, and it hath been seene within half a mile of Horsam; a wonder, no doubte, most terrible and noisome to the inhabitants thereabouts. There is always in his track or path left a glutinous and slimie matter (as by a small similitude we may perceive in a snail's) which is very corrupt and offensive to the scent . . .

This serpent (or dragon, as some call it) is reputed to be nine feete, or rather more, in length, and shaped almost in the forme of an axletree of a cart; a quantitie of thickness in the middest, and somewhat smaller at both endes. The former part, which he shootes forth as a necke, is supposed to be an elle long; with a white ring, as it were, of scales about it. The scales along his backe seem to be blackish, and so much as is discovered under his bellie, appeareth to be red; for I speak of no nearer description than of a reasonable ocular distance. For coming too neare it, hath already beene too dearly paid for, as you shall heare hereafter.

It is likewise discovered to have large feete, but the eye may be there deceived; for some suppose that serpents have no feete . . . [He] rids away (as we call it) as fast as a man can run. He is of countenance very proud, and at the sight or hearing of men or cattel, will raise his neck upright, and seem to listen and looke about, with great arrogancy. There are likewise upon either side of him discovered, two great bunches so big as a large foote-ball, and (as some thinke) will in time grow to wings; but God, I hope, will (to defend the poor people in the neighbourhood) that he shall be destroyed before he grow so fledge.

He will cast his venome about four rodde from him, as by woefull experience it was proved on the bodies of a man and woman coming that way, who afterwards were found dead, being poysoned and very much swelled, but not prayed upon. Likewise a man going to chase it and, as he imagined, to destroy it with two mastive dogs, as yet not knowing the great danger of it, his dogs were both killed, and he himselfe glad to return with haste to preserve his own life. Yet this is to be noted, that the dogs were not prayed upon, but slaine and left whole; for his food is thought to be, for the most part, in a conie-warren, which he much frequents; and it is found much scanted and impaired in the increase it had woont to afford.

The persons, whose names are hereunder printed, have seene this serpent, besides divers others, as the carrier of Horsam, who lieth at the White Horse in Southwark, and who can certifie the truth of all that has been here related.

John Steele
Christopher Holder
and a Widow Woman dwelling neare Faygate.

It is a moot point whether this curious document should be classed as folklore at all. Its details are so sober and circumstantial that one ought probably to look for a naturalistic explanation of the affair, rather than putting it down to superstitious beliefs in dragons, however much these may have been present in the minds of the frightened people of the area. Sheila Kaye-Smith has suggested that a large serpent had escaped from someone's private menagerie, and had been observed at a moment when it was distended by an undigested rabbit – hence the 'thickness in the middest'. Alternatively, to account for the feet and the 'two great bunches', one might interpret the description to fit one of the very large tropical lizards with a frill at the neck. In either case, the unfortunate creature could hardly have survived the winter, and soon it was only a memory, reinforcing the widespread belief in the existence of dangerous and fantastic reptiles.

Discussing the St Leonard's Forest legends in 1861, the antiquarian Mark Anthony Lower noted that in his own boyhood it was still commonly believed that the area was a haunt of monstrous snakes; in his opinion, the idea had been deliberately encouraged by smugglers and gamekeepers, who had reasons of their own to want to keep people away from the woods – 'Beware of Adders' has always been a far more effective notice than 'Private, Keep Out'! Similarly, Charlotte Latham found that the villagers of Fittleworth in 1867 were frightened of an 'audacious large snake', which, they maintained, used to rush out hissing at anyone who passed its lair, and that at Offington there was a belief in fearsome supernatural serpents alleged to be guarding treasure in an underground tunnel under Cissbury.

Even ordinary snakes were quite often credited with strange powers. Thus the adder, which was of course thought (on Scriptural authority) to be deaf, was said to have markings on its belly that read:

> If I could hear as well as see,
> No mortal man should master me.

Another common belief, which was still current a few decades ago and may not yet have died out, was that any snake or worm that is cut in two will not be able to die till sunset. Snakes and snake-oil were used in various folk-medicines, and to kill the first adder you saw in spring was sometimes held to be a charm for ensuring victory. There was also a strong and widespread superstitious fear of snakes – so much so that as late as 1936 there were public protests that the erection of a large caduceus on the façade of the newly opened East Grinstead Hospital would bring bad luck to the district.

The dragon, as portrayed in many local folk-legends in England, is often simply a very large and destructive snake or 'worm', rather than the winged, fire-spewing, fantastic monster of literary epics and romances. One such, of whom little is remembered, is said to have lived on Bignor Hill, where the marks of his coils were still to be seen winding round the hillside – a reference, apparently, to the curving sheep-tracks which were often a noticeable feature of Downland slopes in the days of free-grazing flocks. But the other, and better known, Sussex dragon is said to have been a water-monster (like the Lambton Worm, the Loch Ness Monster, and various other such creatures in British lore). He was called the Knucker, and both he and his dwelling-place, the Knucker Hole at Lyminster, are of considerable interest.

Knucker Hole is a deep pool near Lyminster Church, fed by a strong underground spring, so that though a vigorous stream flows out from it, no water can be seen flowing in. For the same reason, the pool never dries up, and has various other striking and apparently mysterious characteristics. A writer in *Notes and Queries* in 1855 observed that this pond, and some others like it,

> are called by the people thereabouts Nuckar Holes. They are very deep, and considered bottomless, because such strong springs arise in them that they never require to be . . . emptied and cleaned out. A mystery . . . attaches to them among the common people, who seem to have a vague notion of their connexion with another bottomless pit.

In actual fact, this particular pool is only about thirty feet deep, but the story goes that the men of Lyminster once took the six bellropes from their church tower, tied them end to end, and still could not touch the bottom. Other Sussex pools once had a similar reputation, and indeed in some cases shared the same name, though the Lyminster one is now, as far as I know, the only one where the old name is still used. It was also used of 'swallow-holes', i.e. places where streams vanish underground. Miss Helena Hall, whose expanded edition of Parish's *Dictionary of Sussex Dialect* was published in 1957, there defines 'knucker-holes' or 'nucker-holes' as

> springs which rise in the flatlands of the South Downs. They keep at one level, are often twenty feet or so across, and are reputed to be bottomless. The water is cold in summer, but never freezes; in a frost it gives off a vapour, being warmer that the air. Knucker-holes are found at Lyminster, Lancing, Shoreham, Worthing, and many other flats.

The Lancing pool in question may be that near the Sussex Pad, long known to boys of Lancing College as 'the bottomless pond', and Angmering too could be added to the list. All these lie south of the Downs, but the general idea of bottomless pools is not unknown inland; indeed, a correspondent in the *Sussex County Magazine* in 1935 wrote that, thanks to the notions of a nanny from Ashdown Forest, she believed as a child that the whole countryside was full of ponds that went straight through to Australia.

But even more remarkable is the word Knucker or Nucker itself, for it undoubtedly is descended from the Anglo-Saxon *nicor*, 'a water monster'. Originally, presumably, every knucker-hole had its Knucker, a fearsome creature of the Otherworld haunting the 'bottomless' depths. The Anglo-Saxon epic *Beowulf* twice describes *nicoras*, once as fish-like monsters of the open sea, and once as creatures of the same type as our Knucker, 'water-dragons', beings 'of serpent race', living in an eerie pool of immense depth that led straight down to the Otherworld of ogres.

There are words related to *nicor* in Scandinavian languages too, and there they refer to various types of supernatural beings in human or animal form to be found in rivers or lakes. One of these, the Icelandic *nykur*, is a water-horse exactly like the Scottish kelpie in behaviour, and monsters of this type are not unknown in Sussex lore as well. Once again, the legend is associated with a large, deep pool on the coastal plain, this time near Rye; two elderly sisters from Rye used to tell, in the 1920s, how their parents had once seen the creature:

Their father and mother . . . when courting, went for a walk one evening with a dog. They were in a field when a strange creature like a horse came galloping past them. It had the face of a man, and great eyes like saucers. The thunder of the galloping sound seemed to shake the earth. The young man tried to send the dog after it, but he was terrified and would not go. Nothing would induce him to stir. So the young man, leaving the girl, himself followed the creature, when it jumped a high fence and went padding down into a large deep pool just below Mountsfield.

To revert to the story of the Lyminster Knucker, who, unlike this fearsome water-horse, eventually came to a bad end, as most dragons do. For many years he ravaged the countryside for miles around, carrying off cattle, sheep and men, and devouring them in his inaccessible haunts among the marshes of the Arun valley. The devastation grew so dire, and every attempt to dislodge the monster failed so miserably, that at length the King of Sussex offered his daughter's hand to anybody who could kill the Knucker. Even for this reward, few would try. At last, some say, a wandering stranger, a knight errant, killed the dragon in a heroic combat, married the princess, and settled down in Lyminster. There, in the course of time, he died, and there his gravestone can be seen to this day.

This stone is, in fact, a medieval tombstone; it has no inscription, but has a very worn design in which a battered full-length Cross is superimposed on a herring-bone pattern – this, so local tradition asserts, represents the hero's sword laid across the dragon's ribs. The tombstone formerly lay in the graveyard near the church porch, but has now been brought inside the church to save it from further weathering.

But not everybody agrees that the hero who slew the Knucker was a wandering knight. On the contrary, there were some who strongly maintained that he was a local man, either a farmer's boy from Lyminster itself, called Jim Pulk, or 'a young chap from Wick' called Jim Puttock. Nor did he face his foe in open combat, but outwitted him by coolness and cunning, as befits a true Sussex man, who is by no means silly.

Take the story of Jim Pulk first, as told in the 1930s by John Bishop, the gardener at Church Field, Lyminster. When he decided to kill the dragon, he first baked a huge Sussex pie, put poison in it, and drew it on a farm cart near to the Knucker Hole, while he himself hid behind a hedge. The dragon came up out of the water, sniffed the pie, ate the pie, the cart, the horses and all, and very soon afterwards curled up and died. Once he was quite dead, Jim Pulk came out from behind the hedge, and cut off his head with his scythe. He then, so the story goes, went to the Six Bells Inn, had a drink to celebrate his victory, and fell down dead. (Presumably he had unwittingly got some of the poison on his hand, and then, very properly, drawn his hand across his mouth after downing his pint, with disastrous results.) He was buried in the churchyard, under the gravestone already described; at least one child in the 1930s, impressed by the tale, used to deck the stone with snapdragons.

The version of the story with Jim Puttock as the hero was

printed by Charles G. Joiner in the *Sussex County Magazine* in 1929, as told to him by a man from Toddington, whom he met trimming a hedge somewhere near Knucker Hole. It has much in common with the story of Jim Pulk (though not the tragic ending), but also interesting differences and additions; moreover, it is one of the few Sussex legends to have been written down more or less as spoken, with all the raciness of first-class oral story-telling.

Knucker, said the hedger, was a great dragon who lived in the pool 'dunnamany years ago'. Not only would he snap up cows, horses and men for his supper, but he would go swimming in the Arun 'sticking his ugly face up agin the winders in Shipyard when people was sitting having their tea', till the Mayor of Arundel offered a large reward to anyone who would put an end to the Knucker.

So this Jim Puttock, he goes to Mayor and tells him his plan. And Mayor he says everybody must give 'en what he asks, and never mind the expense, 'cause they oughter be thankful anyway for getting rid of the Knucker.

So he goos to the smith and horders a gert iron pot – 'bout *so* big. And he goos to the miller and asks him for so much flour. And he goos to the woodman and tells 'en to build a gert stack-fire in the middle of the Square. And when 'twas done, he set to and made the biggest pudden that was ever seen.

And when 'twas done – not that 'twas quite done – bit sad in the middle, I reckon, but that was all the better, like – they heaved 'en onto a timber-tug, and somebody lent 'en a team to draw it, and off he goos, bold as a lion.

All the people followed 'en as far as the [Arundel] bridge, but they dursn't goo no furder, for there was ole Knucker, lying just below Bill Dawes'es. Least, his head was, but his neck and body-parts lay all along up the hill, past the station, and he was a-tearing up the trees in Batworth Park with his tail.

And he sees thisyer tug a-coming, and he sings out, affable-like, 'How do, Man?'

'How do, Dragon,' says Jim.

'What you got there?' says Dragon, sniffing.

'Pudden,' says Jim.

'Pudden?' says Dragon. 'What be that?'

'Just you try,' says Jim.

And he didn't want no more telling – pudden, horses, tug, they was gone in a blink. Jimmy 'ud 'a gone too, only he hung on to one of they trees what blew down last year.

' 'Tweren't bad,' says Knucker, licking his lips.

'Like another?' says Jim.

'Shouldn't mind,' says he.

'Right,' says Jim, 'Bring 'ee one 'sarternoon.' But he knew better'n that, surelye.

Fore long, they hears 'en rowling about and roaring and bellering fit to bust hisself. And as he rowls, he chucks up gert clods, big as houses, and trees and stones and all manner, he did lash so with his tail. But that Jim Puttock, he weren't afeared, not he. He took a gallon or so with his dinner, and goes off to have a look at 'en.

When he sees 'en coming, ole Knucker roars out: 'Don't you dare bring me no more o' that 'ere pudden, young marn!'

'Why?' says Jim. 'What's matter?'

'Collywobbles,' says Dragon. 'It do set so heavy on me I can't stand up, nohows in the wurreld.'

'Shouldn't bolt it so,' says Jim, 'but never mind, I got a pill here, soon cure that.'

'Where?' says Knucker.

'Here,' says Jim, and he ups with an axe he'd hid behind his back, and cuts off his head.

That's all, but if you goos through that liddle gate there into the churchyard, you'll see Jim's grave.

4 Graves and Ghosts

THE FASCINATION DEATH HOLDS for the imagination is reflected in innumerable tales of haunted houses, churches, churchyards, crossroads, woods and battlefields, of which Sussex, like every other county, has a goodly stock. Not that it has as many now as it once had; even in the 1860s, Lower was commenting on how many had been forgotten since his boyhood days, when:

Nearly every unfrequented corner had its demon in the form of a black dog, while under every sequestered wooden bridge an old woman without a head was supposed to be engaged with her spinning wheel. In the droveway between Kingston (near Lewes) and the marshes of the Ouse, one 'goblin damned' was doomed to a penance more hopeless even that that of Sisyphus, or the Danaides, or of him who had to make a rope of sand; for his ever-unaccomplished labour was, under the figure of a black calf, to spin charcoal incessantly!

But though they may be fewer now, ghost stories are with us

still and seem unlikely to die out. What is noticeable is a certain
change in fashions: it is safe to say that such grotesque horrors
as spinning calves and capering skeletons (see p 123) are now
extinct, that black dogs and headless horsemen are getting rarer,
and that the general trend for many decades has been towards more
dignified and elusive phantoms – footfalls and tappings, bodiless
voices, dim shapes or intangible presences – towards the 'psychic
manifestation', in short, and away from the robust rural taste for
the horrific.

An account of a 'psychic experience', if given at first hand by
the person concerned, with full belief and with the aim of
accuracy, cannot of course be called a folktale; the shaping force
of tradition has not had time to influence it, and (in theory at
least) the teller is not trying to impress or entertain, or to 'make
a good story of it'. On the other hand, a personal account might
sometimes become a starting-point for the growth of a local
legend; passing from mouth to mouth, it might acquire shapeliness
and dramatic force, and as the original 'experience' faded into the
background, the story based on it might come to conform more
and more to some general pattern of what a ghost-story should
be. Moreover, since the idea of ghosts is still accepted by many as
credible, it might at any moment be reinforced by some fresh
'experience'. In short, this is a sphere in which one man's tale may
be the next man's truth. In selecting from the available material,
I have chosen tales which show signs of having circulated long
and widely, and particularly those which show traditional motifs
and story-patterns.

There is nothing that makes so good a focus for a legend as a
conspicuous grave, particularly if there is something eccentric
about it, or about its occupant. One excellent specimen is the
Miller's Tomb, which stands in splendid isolation on the flank
of Highdown Hill, west of Worthing. It was built by John Oliver,
an eighteenth-century miller, in his own lifetime, and the proud
owner used to visit it daily, allegedly to meditate. Local opinion,
both then and now, is divided in its judgement of him; some take
his piety at face-value, but many hold that he was a rogue, in
league with smugglers, and used the hill as a look-out post, the
mill as a means of signalling, and the famous tomb as a hiding-
place for contraband. Be that as it may, when he died in 1793
he had a flamboyant funeral (the coffin was carried by young
girls in white, a custom normally reserved for the burial of very

young and hence incontestably sinless children!); his elaborate
tomb, engraved with many verses, has remained a favourite picnic
spot to this day.

Two legends have developed round the Miller's Tomb. One
is that John Oliver arranged to be buried upside down, because he
believed that at the Last Judgment the whole world would turn
topsy-turvy, and he wanted to be the only man facing the right
way after this upheaval. This weird idea is known elsewhere in
Sussex too; north of Pulborough stands Toat Tower, a tall,
isolated folly built in 1827, and a local story alleges that there is
a man buried under it upside down, together with his horse, which
is also upside down.

The second legend about the Miller's Tomb is that if you run
around it seven times, John Oliver's ghost will jump out and
chase you; it is even asserted that the verses on the tomb (now very
worn) say that this will happen. In fact, of course, they say nothing
of the sort, but are simply the ordinary type of pious verse popular
at that period. One group, on the end slab, is surmounted by a
carving of Time and Death, the latter shown as a skeleton, and
contains the lines:

> Why start you at that skeleton?
> 'Tis your own image that you shun;
> Alive it did resemble thee,
> And thou when dead like that shalt be.

Clearly, these lines and the accompanying picture served as
starting-point for this not very serious tale of ghost-raising.

Equally picturesque and equally baseless is the story attached
to the odd burial-place of 'Mad Jack' Fuller in Brightling churchyard. Fuller, who died in 1834, was a rich and colourful eccentric,
kindly, but with a reputation for wildness; one of his pet pastimes
was building obelisks, mock temples, spires, and other follies. He
had a mausoleum built for him in his lifetime, in the form of a
huge pyramid, an unchristian design which may have been
thought shocking. At any rate, tradition firmly maintains that his
mummified body is sitting bolt upright inside it, on an iron chair,
with his top hat on, and with a bottle of claret on a table in front
of him. Some people add that the floor is all covered with broken
glass, so that if the Devil should come to fetch him away he could
not get near, for fear of cutting his hoof. But Mad Jack's ghost

is not said to walk; with the claret to keep him happy, why should he bother?

The most ancient visible graves in the county are, naturally enough, the prehistoric burial mounds here and there on the Downs, some being Neolithic long barrows, and others Bronze Age round barrows. In a few cases, folk tradition has preserved an awareness that such mounds were burial-places, but it is always wildly astray in its ideas as to who was buried in them, when, and why. It may think of them as graves of giants who lived 'once upon a time' (see pp 28, 30), or of men killed in some relatively modern battle. For instance, the barrows on Mount Harry, near Lewes, are said to cover those who fell in the battle between Henry III and Simon de Montfort in 1264; and two separate groups of barrows at Uppark are said to contain, one the men, and the other the horses, killed in a minor fray during the Civil War.

A striking site reputed haunted as a result of 'battles long ago' is Kingley Vale, north-west of Chichester. Here a narrow coombe is filled from end to end by a magnificent grove of sombre yews, some exceedingly old, while above, on the crest of Bow Hill, stand four large Bronze Age barrows called either The Kings' Graves or The Devil's Humps. These kings, so the tale goes, were leaders of a Viking warband wiped out by the men of Chichester – a battle between men from Chichester and marauding Danes is in fact recorded in *The Anglo-Saxon Chronicle* for 894. The Vikings, or at any rate their leaders, are said to lie in the barrows, and the grove of yews to be descended from trees planted to mark the battlefield. Indeed, many versions of the story prefer to ignore the barrows on the hill, and say that the Danes lie where they fell, under the roots of the yews, and that their ferocious ghosts haunt the dark and silent wood. Others, while agreeing that the wood is haunted, say that its ghosts are those of Druids, and that somewhere, amid all the yews, there stands a single sacrificial oak. And there are yet others who add that in the night the trees themselves can come alive, and move and change their shapes.

Many ghost legends reflect the potted version of history, both national and local, which has survived in the communal memory. A Sussex list would include the following, besides the Danes of Kingley Vale: a Roman centurion haunts the Castle Inn, Chichester; at Chanctonbury Ring, one can raise Julius Caesar and his army by counting the trees, or see an old white-bearded man variously explained as a Druid or as a Saxon killed at the Battle of Hastings; on the site of this great battle, the ground runs red with blood after every shower of rain, and the ghost of the first man killed rides across the field on the anniversary; famished children that beg in the streets of Bramber are said to be the grandsons of the medieval Baron William de Braose, who were starved to death while held hostage at Windsor by King John; at the former Priory of the Hospitallers at Poling, now a private house, one can hear ghostly organ music and Gregorian chant; at Winchelsea, George and Joseph Weston, notorious local highwaymen hanged at Tyburn in 1782, now haunt their former haunts; in the attic of the Red Lion Inn at Hooe, phantom smugglers still mill snuff from contraband tobacco. Doubtless many others could be added to the list.

But ghosts of historical personages, interesting though they are, are not usually very striking in their manifestations, nor do they seem ever to have caused much fear. Some purely local ghosts are described far more vividly, and seem to have once caused considerable alarm, even if only within a few miles' radius. Early in the nineteenth century, for example, there was said to be a most unpleasant spectre in St Leonard's Forest; it was a headless phantom which would lurk among the trees at dusk waiting for some horseman to pass by, and would then spring up behind him, wind its skeletal arm round his neck, and cling to him in spite of all his struggles and pleadings until he reached the further side of the Forest. Howard Dudley, the first writer to mention the ghost, 1836, says it was locally called 'Squire Paulett', and Lower suggests, very tentatively, that this name may refer to a Captain William Powlett who died in 1746. Lower also notes that genuine belief in the ghost was fading in his time (1861), and so we may safely assume that although this spectre continues to live on in guide-books, it is many generations since it was a real cause of fear to travellers in the Forest.

The skulls at Warbleton Priory, on the other hand, were regarded with awe in quite recent times. These are two skulls kept in the Priory ruins (now part of a farm), and the story was that if anyone tried to move them from their place, let alone bury them, ghastly noises would break out in the night, the cattle would fall sick, and ill-luck would befall the hand that moved them. They are said to be the skulls of a former owner of the priory, foully murdered, and of the murderer; needless to say, there was an indelible bloodstain on the floor of the room where the murder took place. As late as 1947, a writer in the *Sussex County Magazine* found the legend very much alive, although he had also spoken with an old lady who had held the skulls in her lap for a full twenty minutes when she was a little girl without suffering any ill-effects or causing any calamities. Indeed, he also tells how the skulls were once taken out of doors and lodged in an apple tree, the only result of this profanation being that a blue tit built its nest in one of them, using the eye-socket as an entrance.

The prize for the most fantastic ghost in Sussex ought, I think, to be equally divided between Rye and Crowborough. The Rye story concerns an oddly-named street, Turkey Cock Lane, near the site of a former monastery. Long ago, it is said, one of the monks fell in love with a girl living near by, and charmed her by his lovely singing; they ran away together, but were caught, and he was buried alive beyond the town walls, whereupon she died of a broken heart. Their ghosts still meet in the lane, and he still tries to sing to her – but his punishment continues in the afterlife, for his fine voice has turned into a turkey's gobble. As for Crowborough, there was a story current there late in the nineteenth century that Jarvis Brook Road was haunted by (of all things) a spectral bag of soot. On certain nights the bag would appear and pursue people walking in the road; once it chased a blacksmith who had defied it all the way to his own home.

A story from Cuckfield has several points of interest. It concerns a member of one of the wealthy local families, Mrs Ann Pritchard Sergison, who died in 1848 at the age of 85. She had been a redoubtable old lady, notorious for her vindictive temper, which came out in bitter feuds with her tenants and even with her own son; indeed, she was locally known as 'Wicked Dame Sergison'. Soon after her death, rumours began :

The country people said she was too wicked to rest in her grave, and ghost stories about her grew up. Carters on the road from Cuckfield to Ansty declared that their horses shied at the sight of her ghost swinging on the oak gates at the entrance to Cuckfield Park, and people became afraid to travel on this road at night. Finally three clergymen, the vicar and curate of Cuckfield and the vicar of Balcombe, are said to have held a service of exorcism in Cuckfield Church at midnight. Gossips reported that they had caused the ghost to drown in the font.

However that may be, the ghost stopped haunting the highway, and soon after her son replaced the oak gates by iron ones with spikes.

This story is more shapely than most, beginning with some indication of the type of character to whom the haunting is attributed, and ending with the laying of the ghost. Many traditional tales, especially in the west of England, end with the exorcism of the ghost to some lonely pool, or far away to the Red Sea; the mention of a font for the purpose is unusual, and is perhaps an echo of Catholic belief in the efficacy of Holy Water. Other incidental details show authentic folk-beliefs, for instance in the well-known power of iron against all evil spirits, and in the ghost's choice of a gate for its manifestations; gateways and stiles often figure in folklore as haunted spots, the idea probably being that boundaries and points of intersection are places where supernatural forces may more easily break through into the normal world.

Ghostly animals are a common theme in folklore, the most usual being dogs and horses, plus the occasional calf (see pp 23, 43, 51). It is not always clear whether such creatures are thought of as ghosts of dead animals, as purely otherworld creatures which had never walked this earth in flesh and blood, or even sometimes as ghosts of human beings reappearing in animal form. The best-known Sussex tradition of a ghostly dog dates from the nineteenth century and concerns the road between Alfriston and Seaford; it was said that a white dog used to appear there on Midsummer Eve every seven years, and brought death or disaster to anyone who saw it. The story is associated with the discovery of a man's skeleton at the roadside when the road was widened early in the nineteenth century; it was alleged that this was the body of the 'long-lost heir' of one of the local families (which one is not clear) who had been murdered by robbers, together with his faithful dog, some time in the eighteenth century. Some versions of the story stress the man's ghost, which haunted his rightful home; others that of the dog, which is said never to have appeared again after its master's body had been found.

The Alfriston dog was visible to men, but it was also once commonly believed that 'the ghosts of dogs occasionally walk abroad, unheard, unseen, except by their own species', and that if dogs bark inexplicably and persistently, it is a sign that they

D

are disturbed by the sight of their ghostly counterparts. On the other hand, the black dogs which Lower declares were once to be found in every unfrequented corner are classified by him as demons, not as ghosts; there is still a vague tradition of a headless black dog haunting Black Dog Hill, on the road between Ditchling and Westmeston, but there is nothing to cast light on its nature or the reason for its presence.

Definitely demonic are the spectral packs of 'wish hounds' or 'witch hounds'; as late as the 1930s it was possible to find Downland shepherds who claimed that they, or more often their sheepdogs, had heard them sweeping past overhead, as they hunted the souls of the damned through the sky. The great windswept height of Ditchling Beacon is said to be the site of such a spectral hunt; one can hear the cry of the hounds, the horses' hooves, and the huntsman's horn, but nothing is ever to be seen. The belief can lend itself to deliberate exploitation; round Fairlight Cove, smugglers and their allies used to fill the ears of credulous folk with tales about 'wind hounds', fierce unearthly creatures that raced along the cliffs on certain nights – the nights when cargoes were due to be landed.

Smugglers did a great deal to foster all sorts of ghost stories as a cover for their activities. It is widely believed that the famous eighteenth-century 'Drummer of Hurstmonceux', a spectre sometimes described as being nine feet tall, which filled the nights with eerie drum-beats, was a signalman for the local smuggling gang, and it was noticed that once the preventive men had restored the rule of law in this part of Sussex, the manifestations ceased. Occasionally tricks of this sort were unmasked on the spot by some resolute investigator, as in an incident as Edburton early in the nineteenth century:

> One morning the whole place was in consternation, owing to a report that two men had been frightened close to a large wood by a ghost, which appeared in the shape of an animal about the size of a calf, with two flaming eyes. Everyone was afraid to go near the place. Mr Thomas Marshall . . . went and examined it, and found a large quantity of smuggled goods.

So much for the legendary ghosts of old Sussex; but the modern age has evolved some widely-circulating stories of its own, each with its own typical pattern, and at least one of these, 'the

Phantom Hitch-Hiker', has cropped up in a Sussex setting. A motorist, so the story goes, gave a lift to a girl who was hitching southwards on the London to Worthing road. As he passed through Horsham, he felt a great longing for a cup of coffee, so he stopped at a wayside café; the girl refused to get out, so he left her sitting in the car. When he came back, she had disappeared, and he could find nobody who had seen what became of her. He was so worried over what might have happened to her that he decided to telephone her parents (for she had mentioned their address); to his horror, he learnt that their only daughter had been killed three years before, run over while hitching a lift outside a Horsham café.

5 Fairies

ALTHOUGH IT IS MOST IMPROBABLE that a belief in fairies is seriously held by any adult of the present generation, it was a different matter in the nineteenth century, when anecdotes based on this once quite general belief were still circulating fairly widely. Even one generation ago, it was not utterly extinct. A contributor to the *Sussex County Magazine* in 1954 described how, during her childhood on a farm near Chiddingly a labourer named Harry used to tell her how:

> The little 'pharisees' helped a sick workman by thrashing out his corn for him while he slept, until he woke to hear one little man say to his companion, 'I twet; do you twet?' [i.e. sweat], and the sick man burst out laughing, which so offended the pharisees that they never helped him again. This and other stories he told us, not so much to amuse us, as to warn us never to offend these little people, whom he firmly believed in and said he had seen when he was at work in the woods.

The tale Harry told is a common one, earlier and fuller versions of which will be given below – what is interesting is his attitude to the faires, whom he thinks of as living in close daily contact with men, and as being both helpful, up to a point, and also potentially dangerous if offended. This is firmly in the main line of English fairy legends (as opposed to the more fanciful nursery tales); as the writer shrewdly notes, Harry told his stories 'not to amuse us, but to warn'.

The term 'pharisees', incidentally, is not so inexplicable as it may appear. A feature of Sussex dialect, as of several others, is the reduplicated plural such as 'waspses' or 'ghostses'; by this process, 'fairies' became 'fairises', and this in turn came to be confused with the Biblical Pharisees, in pronunciation at least.

The Sussex fairy beliefs are excellently illustrated by two cautionary tales which the antiquary M. A. Lower published in 1854, they having been told him by a countryman named William Fowington, who had turned seventy at the time. Lower regarded them as mere survivals of stories current in the eighteenth century (Will Fowington having set them three generations before his own time), but it will be seen that the second is the full version of the story Harry was still telling early in this century, about the sweating fairies. Lower took pains to render Will Fowington's tales in his own words, thus providing us with a vivid example of rural narrative art from well over a hundred years ago:

When I was a liddle boy and lived with my gurt uncle, old Jan Duly, dere was a old place dey used to call Burlow Castle [i.e. the earthwork, probably a medieval fort, near Arlington]. It warn't much ov a castle – onny a few old walls like – but it had been a famous place in de time when dere was a king in every county. Well, whatever it had been afore, at the time I speak on, it was de very hem [hell] of a place for Pharisees, and nobody didn't like to goo by it ahter dark for fear on um.

One dee as Chols Packham, uncle's grandfather (I've heerd uncle tell de story a dunna-many times) was at plough up dere, jest about cojer time [i.e. lunch break], he heerd a queer sort of a noise right down under de groun' dat frightened him uncommonly, sure-lie. 'Hullow,' says Chols to his mate, 'did you hear dat, Harry?' 'Yahs,' says Harry, 'what was it?' 'I reckon 'twas a Pharisee,' says uncle's grandfather. 'No 'twarn't,' says Harry, 'dere aren't no Pharisees now. Dere was *once* – at Jerusalem; but dey was full-growed people, and has been dead hunderds o' years.'

Well, while dey was a-talking, Chols heerd de noise agin – 'Help! Help! Help!' Chols was terribly afeard, but he plucked up heart enough to ax what was wanted.

'I've been a-bakin',' said de liddle voice, 'and have broke my peel' (dat's a sort o' thing dat's used to put loaves into de oven wid), 'and I dunno what upon de airth to do.'

Under de airth, Chols thought she ought to ha' said, but howsomever he didn't say so. And being a tender-hearted kind of a chap dat didn't like anybody to be in trouble, he made answer without any preamble, 'Put it up, and I'll try to mend it.'

No sooner said dan done; dere was a chink in de groun', for de season was dryish, and sure enough, through dat chink dere come up a liddle peel not bigger dan a bren-cheese knife. Chols couldn't hardly help laughin', it was such a monstrous *liddle* peel, not big enough to hold a gingey-bread nut hardly; but howsomever he thought 'twas too seerous a thing to laugh at, for he knowed of old how dahngerous 'twas to offend any of dem liddle customers. So he outs wud a tin-tack or two as he happened to have in his weskit pocket, and wud de help ov his cojer knife for a hammer, and his knee for a bench, he soon mended de peel and put it down de chink.

Harry was back-turned while dis was a-gooin' on, and when he come back Chols up and told him all about it; but Harry said 'twas all stuff, and he didn't believe a word consarnin' on't, for Master Pettit, de parish clerk, had told him 'twas all a galushon [delusion], and dere warn't no Pharisees nowadays.

But howsomever he proved to be wrong more ways dan one, for next dee at cojer time when Harry was back-turned agin, Chols Packham heerd de voice as afore a-comin' up out ov de chink, and a-sayin', 'Look here!'

Well, Chols turned roun', not quite so much frightened dis time, and what should he see standin' close agin de chink but a liddle bowl full of summat dat smelled a hem-an'-all better dan small beer.

'Hullow!' thinks Chols to hisself, 'dis is worth havin',' he thinks. So he tasted it, and at last drunk it all up; and he 'llowed dat of all de stuff *he* ever tasted, dat was de very best.

He was a-gooin' to save de liddle bowl to show Harry dat dere
certainly *was* fairies, but whilst he was a-thinking about it, all
of a sudden de bowl slipped out of his hands and dashed itself
into a hundred pieces, so dat Harry onny laughed at him, and
said 'twas naun but a cracked basin.

But howsomever, Harry got sarved out for bein' so
unbelievin', for he fell into a poor way, and couldn't goo to
work as usual, and he got so tedious bad, dat he fell away to
mere skin and boän and no doctors couldn't do him no good,
and dat very day twelmont he died, at de very same hour dat de
Pharisees was fust heerd, and dat he spoke agin 'em.

An ol' brother of my wife's gurt granmother *see* some
Pharisees once, and 'twould ha' been a power better if so be he
hadn't never seen 'em, or leastways never offended 'em. I'll
tell ye how it happened. Jeems Meppom – dat was his naüm –
Jeems was a liddle farmer, and used to thresh his own corn. His
barn stood in a very elenge [i.e. dreary] lonesome place, a
goodish bit from de house, and de Pharisees used to come dere
a nights and thresh out some wheat and wuts [i.e. oats] for
him, so dat de hep o' threshed corn was ginnerly bigger in de
morning dan what he left it overnight.

Well, ye see, Mas' Meppom thought dis a liddle odd, and
didn't rightly know what to make on't. So, bein' an out-and-
out bold chep, dat didn't fear man nor devil, as de sayin' is, he
made up his mind dat he'd goo over some night to see how
'twas managed.

Well, accordingly he went out rather airly in de evenin', and
laid up behind de mow [straw stack] for a long while, till he
got rather tired and sleepy, and thought 'twaunt no use a-
watchin' no longer. It was gettin' pretty handy to midnight, and
he thought how he'd goo home to bed. But jest as he was upon
de move, he heerd a odd sort of a soun' comin' toe-ards de
barn, and so he stopped to see what it was. He looked out of
de strah [straw], and what should he catch sight on but a couple
of liddle cheps about eighteen inches high or dereaway come
into de barn without uppening de doors. Dey pulled off dere
jackets and begun to thresh wud two liddle frails as dey had
brought wud 'em, at de hem of a rate.

Mas' Meppom would ha' been froughten if dey had been
bigger, but as dey was such tedious *liddle* fellers, he couldn't
hardly help bustin' right out a-laffin'. Howsomever, he pushed

a handfull of strah into his mouth and so managed to kip quiet a few minutes a-lookin' at 'em – thump, thump; thump, thump; as riglar as a clock.

At last dey got rader tired and left off to rest derselves, and one on 'em said, in a liddle squeakin' voice, as it might ha' bin a mouse a-talkin': 'I say, Puck, I tweat; do you tweat?'

At dat, Jeems couldn't contain hisself no-how, but set up a loud haw-haw; and jumpin' up from de strah hollered out: 'I'll tweat ye, ye liddle rascals! What bisness ha' you got in my barn?'

Well upon dis, de Pharisees picked up der frails and cut away right by him, and as dey passed by him he felt sich a queer pain in his head as if somebody had gi'en him a lamentable hard thump wud a hammer, dat knocked him down as flat as a flounder. How long he laid dere he never rightly knowed, but it must ha' bin a goodish bit, for when he come to, 'twas gettin' deelight.

He couldn't hardly contrive to doddle home, and when he did he looked so tedious bad dat his wife sent for de doctor dirackly. But bless ye, *dat* waunt no use; and old Jeems Meppom knowed it well enough. De doctor told him to kip up his sperits, beein' 'twas onny a fit he had had from bein' amost smothered wud de handful of strah and kippin' his laugh down. But Jeems knowed better. ' 'Tain't no use, sir', he says, says he, to de doctor, 'de cuss of de Pharisees is uppon me, and all de stuff in your shop can't do *me* no good.'

And Mas' Meppom was right, for about a year ahtewuds he died, poor man, sorry enough dat he'd ever intarfered wud things dat didn't consarn him. Poor ol' feller, he lays buried in de churchaird over yonder – leastways, so I've heerd my wife's mother say – under de bank jest where de bed of snowdraps grows.

This story of the sweating fairies was very widely known. Mrs Latham, writing in 1878, says it was the favourite Sussex fairy tale in the days of her youth, and gives a version from Washington in which the spying farmer offends the little people simply by crying out, 'Well done, my little fellows!' But his punishment is less drastic than poor Jeems Meppom's – the fairies simply vanish, and refuse to help him again.

Or again, there is a variant given by the Rev W. D. Parish of

Selmeston in 1875, of which the hero is a carter, as told him by
a Downland man:

> I've heerd my feäther say that when he lived over the hill, there
> was a carter that worked on the farm along wid him, and no-one
> couldn't think how 'twas that this here man's horses looked so
> much better than what anyone else's did. I've heerd my feäther
> say that they was that fat they couldn't scarcely get about; and
> this here carter he was just as much puzzled as what the rest
> was, so 'cardingly he laid hisself up in the steäble one night,
> to see if he could find the meaning on't.
>
> And he hadn't been there very long before these here liddle
> farises they crep' in at the sink hole; in they crep', one after
> another; liddle tiny bits of chaps they was, and each on 'em had
> a liddle sack of corn on his back, as much as ever he could
> carry. Well! In they crep', on they gets, up they climbs, and
> there they was, just as busy feeding these here horses. And
> prensley [presently] one says to 'tother, he says, 'Puck,' he says,
> 'I twets; do you twet?'
>
> And thereupon this here carter he jumps up and says,
> 'Dannel ye [drat you],' he says, 'I'll make ye twet afore I've done
> wid ye!' But afore he could get anigh them, they was all gone,
> every one on 'em.
>
> And I've heerd my feäther say, that from that day forard
> this here carter's horses fell away, till they got that thin and
> poor that he couldn't bear to be seen along wid 'em, so he took
> and went away, for he couldn't abear to see hisself no longer,
> and nobody ain't seen him since.

The fairies might well manifest themselves in farm dairies as
well as in barns and stables. Here too they would, if left to themselves, be willing to be helpful, but if they were sneered at or
spoken ill of, they would turn mischievous and revenge themselves
by such antics as smashing cream-pans, preventing the butter from
'coming' in the churn, or turning cattle loose. Moreover, the fairies
would disappear if the wrong sort of reward was offered them,
just as their counterparts in other regions, the brownies and pixies,
were said to do; a dish of milk was welcome, but a gift of clothes
would put them to flight. A story collected by Miss Candlin tells
how a helpful fairy named Dobbs always wore a tattered hat; the
grateful farmer set out a new one for him one night, and heard

him exclaim: 'New hat, new hat! Dobbs will do no more good!'
– after which he never came again.

'Dobbs' is a widespread name in Sussex for these domestic
drudging fairies, and there was a common saying, 'I see Master
Dobbs has been helping you', which was used to someone who
has got through a piece of work unexpectedly fast. Dobbs was
particularly invoked by women when their butter would not 'come'
properly; he would help them, if they repeated this charm
three times:

> Come, butter, come!
> Come, butter, come!
> Peter stands at the gate,
> Waiting for a buttered cake.
> Come, butter, come!

Fairies were also said to reward hard-working servant girls by
slipping a small silver coin into their shoes while they were asleep
– presumably it was their mistress who saw to it that this belief
was kept up! In the same way, nowadays, young children are
encouraged to let their mothers pull out their loose milk-teeth
with the promise that if they are good about this, and if they put
the tooth under the pillow, they will find in the morning that
the fairies have taken the tooth away and left a sixpence there
instead.

It was noticed above that the Burlow Castle mentioned in the
first story recorded by Lower is a conspicuous medieval earthwork.
This is by no means the only case of fairies being thought to live in
a spot marked out by some perplexing ancient feature. It is said,
for instance, that they can be seen at midnight on Midsummer
Eve, dancing on Tarberry Hill and on Cissbury, both of which
have hill-forts at the summit; also that a fairy funeral was once
seen on Pulborough Mount (i.e. Park Mound, which has the
ruins of a Norman motte); and that Harrow Hill near Patching,
which has flintmines and earthworks on it, was locally believed
to have been 'the last home of the fairies in England':

> They had a troubled time of it for many years, and got dis-
> satisfied with the ways and goings-on of modern people, and
> at last when scientific diggers came, and cold inquiries were
> made, and some of them proclaimed their cold unbelief and

sniffed when the word 'pharisees' was mentioned, the little people could stand it no more, and all have left.

Despite the feeling, once so prevalent, that fairies are best left alone for fear of offending them, there are one or two prescribed rituals by which those who wish to catch a glimpse of them can do so. There is, however, a certain prettiness about these procedures which probably indicates that they belong to a more recent layer of tradition, where belief in fairies was fast declining into a charming fancy for children.

One, already mentioned, is to go on Midsummer Eve to one or other of the places which they are said to haunt; another is to find a 'fairy ring' in the grass, and run round it nine times on the first night of the new moon, whereupon you will hear their laughter and music coming up from underground. The third is more elaborate, and its provenance is curious. In 1952 a contributor to The *Sussex County Magazine* described the stories and lore with which her nanny had fascinated her in childhood; many of these tales concerned a certain Mrs Jasper whom the nurse had known in her own childhood, who had been reputed to be a witch. This Mrs Jasper had boasted of having a charm to make fairies come, and had demonstrated it to the little girl who later became the nanny:

You had to do it on a moonlight night when the pollen was just ripe on the catkins . . . She stood a few yards away [in a woodland clearing] with two small branches in her hands. I saw the gold dust flying from the catkins as she waved them gently, and she sang a little song over and over in a low drawlin' husky voice – just as though she was coaxin' 'em:

>   Come in the stillness,
>   Come in the night;
>   Come soon,
>   And bring delight.
>   Beckoning, beckoning,
>   Left hand and right;
>   Come *now*,
>   Ah, come tonight!

Finally, an amusing tale which Mrs Latham declares was a popular favourite in Sussex nurseries about a hundred years ago:

There were once two men who stole a fine pig from a farmer's sty, crammed it into a sack, and set off to carry it home. Their way lay up the steep slopes of Beeding Hill. The day was hot, and the pig was heavy, so half way up the hill they put the sack down and stopped for a rest — but they had laid that sack just on top of a fairy's hole. Presently they set out again, and before they had gone very far, the man whose turn it was to carry the sack saw a tiny little figure running along by his side, and heard it call out in a shrill and doleful little voice, 'Dick, Dick, where be you?'

The man was already startled enough, but then he was terrified to hear another voice, from *inside* the sack:

> In a sack,
> Pick-a-back,
> Going up Beeding Hill.

He threw down the sack, and he and his mate ran off as fast as they could. The two fairies nipped back into their hole, and as for the pig, he was already well on his way home to his own sty, back to the farmer — who was a man who was always on good terms with the fairies.

6 The Devil

SATAN, SO SOME PEOPLE SAY, rarely ventures into Sussex because, knowing that good Sussex cooks will make puddings out of pretty well anything, he is afraid of being made a pudding of. All the same, he has left a good many marks on our topography. There is the Devil's Ditch, a six-mile bank and ditch running from near Halnaker to near West Stoke; the Devil's Bog, in Ashdown Forest; the Devil's Road, a local name for the stretch of the old Roman Stane Street that passes through Billingshurst, so called because it is the only flint-made road for miles around, and because it runs so unnaturally straight; the Devil's Dyke, of which more will be said below; the Devil's Book, an earthwork in a valley at the foot of the Caburn; the Devil's Humps, a group of four Bronze Age barrows on Bow Hill; and the Devil's Jumps, a similar group of five barrows on Treyford Hill. As to how these last got their name, the following story is told in the district:

In the old days, the god Thor was fond of sitting on the top of Treyford Hill for a rest. One day the Devil came by, and, seeing the five barrows, he took it into his head to amuse himself leaping through the air from one to another. All this thumping and jumping disturbed Thor, who woke up in a temper, and shouted: 'Go away!'

But Old Nick only laughed and jeered at him. 'Poor old Thor!' he said. 'Don't you wish you could jump like me? But you're too old to go jumping about,' said he.

The words were no sooner out of his mouth than Thor upped with a huge stone and hurled it straight at him. It got him full in the midriff, just as he was in the middle of his finest jump. So the old Devil, he gave a great yell, and he took himself off double quick. And he has never been seen there from that day to this, though of course the mounds are still there.

Satan's contributions to Sussex scenery could be quite sensational. The conspicuously isolated Torbery Hill was formed from a spoon which he flung aside in anguish one day when he had burnt his lips sipping scalding hot punch from his Punch Bowl in Surrey. But the best-known of such legends is that of the Devil's Dyke, a cleft in the Downs to the north of Hove, running south-west from near the village of Poynings towards the sea.

The Devil, so it is said, had been infuriated by the conversion of Sussex, one of the last strongholds of paganism in England, and more particularly by the way the men of the Weald were building churches in all their villages. So he swore that he would dig right through the Downs in a single night, to let in the sea and drown them all. He started just near Poynings and dug and dug most furiously, sending great clods of earth flying left and right – one became Chanctonbury, another Cissbury, another Rackham Hill, and yet another Mount Caburn. Towards midnight, the noise he was making disturbed an old woman, who looked out to see what was going on. As soon as she understood what he was up to, she lit a candle and set it on her window-sill, holding up a sieve in front of it to make a dimly glowing globe. The Devil looked round, and thought this was the rising sun. At first he could hardly believe his eyes, but then he heard a cock crowing – for the old woman, just to make quite sure, had knocked her cockerel off his perch. So Satan flew away, leaving his work half done. Some say that as he went out over the Channel, a great dollop of earth fell from his cloven hoof, and that's how the Isle of Wight was made; others, that he bounded straight over into

Surrey, where the impact of his landing formed the hollow known as his Punch Bowl.

That, at least, is how most Sussex people tell the tale. But there are alternative versions which ascribe the saving of the Weald to a saint, though they disagree as to which one should have the credit. Hilaire Belloc, who retells the story with great verve in *The Four Men*, says that St Dunstan made the Devil agree to finish the work in one night, before cockcrow, and then by the power of his prayers caused all the cocks in the length and breadth of the Weald to crow all together in chorus, though the day had not yet dawned. A guidebook on sale at the Dyke, drawing on Harrison Ainsworth's novel *Ovingdean Grange* (1879), gives the credit jointly to St Cuthman and a fictitious nun, Ursula de Braose, whose prayers afflicted Satan with cramps and whose blessed candle tricked him. Indeed, as early as 1837 there is an allusion in the *Penny Post* saying that he was foiled by a holy hermit and the power of the Cross.

It may be added that two small rectangular mounds at the lower (i.e. northern) end of the Dyke, which are in fact the foundations of disused ox-steddles, are known as the Devil's Grave and the Devil's Wife's Grave – so it would appear that some story-tellers claimed that the fiend died of his exertions.

Another highly popular legend about Satan in Sussex revolves round his epic encounter with St Dunstan at Mayfield; its ultimate source is Eadmar's *Life of St Dunstan,* written ca, 1120, but it has of course grown during the centuries. At the time when Dunstan was Archbishop of Canterbury, Mayfield was his favourite country residence, and it is said that, being a skilled metal-worker, he had a smithy of his own in the Palace grounds. One day, as he was at work making horseshoes (or, some say, a chalice), the Devil came to him disguised as a lovely girl, who began by discussing her spiritual problems, but soon passed on to flirting and amorous advances. Dunstan, guessing the truth, just kept on working quietly at the forge, while she sidled closer and closer. As soon as she was within arm's reach, he snatched his red-hot tongs out of the fire, and caught her by her pretty little nose. She shrieked, and all at once changed into a hideous monster; again and again she changed her shape, each form being more terrifying than the last, but still the saint held on. At last Satan, beaten, appeared in his own form, Dunstan released him, and the wretched fiend flew off as fast as he could to Tunbridge Wells to cool his nose in the waters. They have had a reddish colour and a curious flavour ever since. As for the tongs, they can be seen in the Old Palace at Mayfield (now part of a Convent school) to this very day.

But others say that the Devil flew off while the tongs were still on his nose, and that as Dunstan would by no means let go of them, he too was whirled through the air until he reached the spot known as Dunstan's Bridge, not far from Tunbridge Wells, where he at last relaxed his grip, fell to earth unhurt, and dipped his glowing tongs in the springs at Tunbridge Wells. Others again claim that the Devil cooled his nose in the Roaring Spring, about a mile away from Mayfield, and that once a year these waters roar in memory of the event. There is even a tale that the village of Tongdean, near Brighton, is the place where the tongs fell from Satan's nose, though this is many miles from the scene of action, even as the Devil flies.

Needless to say, Satan could not be expected to accept defeat meekly, and there are two further tales of his attempts to be avenged on Dunstan. The first, about how he tried to spoil the church at Mayfield, has been told already (pp 19–20). The second tells how he did his best to destroy the village itself.

One day, when the Mayfield Convent had just been built, the Devil met St Dunstan and told him that he was going to knock down every house in the village. The saint bargained with him, asking whether he would be willing to leave standing any house that had a horseshoe on it. Now at that time the custom of nailing horseshoes over doorways was quite unknown, so the Devil laughed, and said he would willingly promise that. But Dunstan was a blacksmith, and he knew a thing or two. He rushed round from house to house fixing up a horseshoe on each one, and as he kept just one step ahead of the Devil all the way, Old Nick could do no damage after all.

It must be many centuries since legends such as these commanded any serious belief, but the next group of stories forms a rather different category, being jokes to most, but of more weight to others, particularly children.

For instance, there is a taboo, still fairly widely upheld, against eating blackberries after 10 October, because, they say, during that night the Devil goes by and spits on every bush. It was at one time thought that to break the taboo would bring death or disaster before the year was out; nowadays, it is generally simply said

that the berries never taste nice after this date. It is indeed
a fact that the fruit tends to become watery and flavourless at
about this time, because of the night frosts. However, the precise
choice of date must go back to the period when the English
calendar was adjusted by eleven days in 1752, for 10 October in
the new reckoning corresponds to 29 September in the old, and
this is Michaelmas Day, a feast celebrating the primeval war in
which St Michael the Archangel hurled Lucifer out of Heaven
and down to earth.

There was also an old and semi-serious taboo against picking
nuts on Sundays; if you did, the Devil would come and hold the
branches down for you. This belief was sometimes deliberately
used, some fifty years ago, to stop children from spoiling their
good Sunday clothes; I myself heard it in the 1940s, very seriously
mentioned by a pious girl of about fourteen who was trying to
stop some younger children, myself included, from breaking the
Sabbath in this way. There is also a Sussex saying recorded by Mrs
Latham in the 1860s, and still occasionally to be heard as late as
the Second World War, to the effect that something – for instance
a grubby child, or a dark night – is 'as black as the Devil's
nutting bag'.

The earliest Sussex story involving this belief clearly shows that
it could have frivolous undertones. It is an account of a practical
joke played on some girls in 1814, in Tilehurst Woods, near
Hailsham. It was told by an old woodman, William, to the Rev
Thomas Geering of Hailsham, who included it in his book *Our
Parish* (1884). In those days it was a common belief that if a
girl went nutting on Sunday the Devil would appear to help her,
but Geering pointedly adds that he was expected to make his
appearance in the form of her sweetheart, who would be 'met
and welcomed', would make himself useful, and would carry
her bag of nuts home for her. One can well imagine the opportunities for flirtation to which this agreeable custom would give
rise; it is even possible that in Sussex, as elsewhere, 'going
nutting' was a rural euphemism for making love.

William's story was that one autumn Sunday in 1814 five
young women went nutting in Tilehurst Wood, and as the afternoon wore on they were annoyed to notice that none of their
sweethearts had bothered to turn up. They had piled their nuts
in an open glade, and would scatter among the thickets and then
return to the glade with more bagfuls. Returning from one such

E

foray, they were horrified to see Satan himself squatting on the pile of nuts, coal black and grinning, with scarlet flames leaping round his legs. They screamed and ran, and when one of them heard her name called, they only ran the faster. William happened to meet them in their panic flight, and when he heard their queer story he told them to go home, and leave him to deal with the Devil, and the nuts. But when he got to the glade, it was empty – no Devil, and no nuts.

Next day the bags of nuts were found tossed into somebody's front garden, but the mystery was not much clearer for all that. Only two years later did the explanation emerge, when the Berkshire Militia, who had been quartered in nearby barracks, were due to leave the next day. A tall, jolly Negro soldier, Dan the Drummer, then confessed that he had wanted to play a trick on the girls. He had stripped, and seated himself among the nuts, draping his scarlet tunic over his legs. He had never meant to frighten them so badly, and when he saw how scared they were he realised that to run after them would only make matters worse. He had returned the nuts secretly, and had not dared admit his prank till he was about to leave the district.

Another type of story which may sometimes be believed, at any rate by children, though it is more commonly told as a joke, is that which claims that one can raise the Devil at some particular spot. The basic procedure is simple, merely running round the spot in question, but extra conditions may be added to make the task more difficult, or even impossible. The site may be a prominent landmark, such as the barrows known as the Devil's Humps on Bow Hill; there are four of them, and you must go round six times, so the condition is more taxing than it seems. Or it may be a tree, like one by the old Rectory at Kingston-on-Sea (which is also said to have a man buried under its roots, with a dagger through his heart). It may be an empty building; a writer in the *Sussex County Magazine* in 1953 says that in her childhood she and other children in her village (which she does not name) believed that if they ran three times, very fast, round a neglected old Unitarian Chapel there, and then peered in at the window, they would see Satan sitting there.

Old tombs and family vaults attract similar tales, possibly because in the palmy days of smuggling they afforded such excellent hiding-places for contraband; the smugglers would have an obvious interest in frightening people away from churchyards, and the temptation to make puns about 'raising spirits' at midnight must have been quite irresistible. Be that as it may, at Heathfield, a generation or so ago, children firmly believed that if you ran seven times round the family vault of the Blunts, the Devil would leap out; and the same is said of the Miller's Tomb (see p 45), and also of the oldest tomb in Broadwater Churchyard, Worthing. But here again, frivolity creeps in. In 1968, a Worthing man in his fifties told me that when he was young he and his friends used to take their girls to Broadwater Churchyard at midnight, telling them this legend – 'and I don't say we raised the Devil, exactly,' he said, and broke off, grinning.

One well-known legend of this type concerns Chanctonbury Ring, and it is very much alive. The basic idea is that if you run seven times round this famous clump of trees, the Devil will come from among them, and will offer you a bowl of soup (or, some say, milk, or porridge). Many tellers lay down more specific instructions, ranging from the eerie to the impossible: the circuits must be performed on a moonless night, at seven o'clock on Midsummer Day, at midnight, during the actual time it takes a clock to strike midnight, or (worst of all) you must run round backwards. Some say you should refuse the proffered soup, or Satan will have you in his power; others say nothing about food at all, but simply that he will chase you, possibly to the Devil's Dyke, nine miles away. Some children admit to having been frightened by the tale when they first heard it, and adults with an inclination to believe in the occult have also been known to take it seriously; however, it is far more often told light-heartedly, and received in the same spirit.

There is one Sussex story of devil-raising which belongs in a different category, that of anecdotes about efficient (or inefficient) wizards. The belief that certain men had enough command of magical arts to raise spirits of various types, whether for good or ill, was very generally accepted in England until well on in the seventeenth century; among country people and the uneducated it lingered far longer, though naturally other magic powers, such as those of healing and of laying ghosts, were more frequently in demand. Many villages had 'cunning men' who traded on such beliefs, and local traditions naturally gathered about the more famous of them.

At the end of the nineteenth century, Boys Firmin heard a story about one such in Crowborough. It was said that this man had once raised the Devil in his cottage by Crowborough Green, but having done so, and having obtained from him whatever it was he wanted, he had great difficulty in laying him again. Luckily the wizard's son was at hand, and he had the presence of mind to scatter a whole sackful of clover seed across the floor and to set Satan the task of picking every seed up, one by one. Having thus gained a precious breathing-space, father and son were able to call to mind the correct formulas and ritual, and together they sent the Devil back to his own place.

On the other hand, Mike Mills, a noted smuggler, outwitted Satan by sheer stamina, not by magic arts. The story goes that this man, whose many crimes had made him a likely candidate for damnation, challenged the Devil to a race in St Leonard's Forest, staking his soul against a promise that the fiend would leave him in peace for ever. The race was run along the avenue, a mile and a half in length, which is still known as Mike Mills' Race; Mike won, and so became immortal, for Heaven would not have him, and the Devil had sworn never to touch him.

It will be seen that in almost all these tales in which a personalised Devil appears, he is a figure of fun, easily duped or driven off. The situation is a very different one when he is thought of as a diffuse force of ill-luck, akin to the blighting magic force of the evil eye, responsible for crop failures and inexplicable illnesses. In this aspect, the Devil was a very real source of fear to countrymen, not to be lightly named, and to be kept at bay by various charms – crossed scythes, horseshoes, horse-brasses, and so forth. But such considerations bring us to the verge of the grimmer subject of witch beliefs.

7 Witches

DREAD OF THE POWER of witches was very real in rural life at least until the latter part of the nineteenth century, and anecdotes about alleged witches, together with various pieces of traditional advice on how to foil them, lingered on until modern times. It is indeed noteworthy how often those contributors to the *Sussex County Magazine* who sent in the most detailed accounts of local witches thought it advisable, even in the 1930s and 1940s, to conceal the true names of persons and places, in order to spare the feelings of surviving relatives of the people concerned.

Anecdotes about witches fall into certain recurrent patterns, of which the two most popular concern their ability to turn themselves into hares, and their power to immobilise waggons or other vehicles. It was firmly believed that any witch could turn into a hare as soon as she was alone and unobserved. In proof of this, it was often alleged that the local huntsmen had repeatedly sighted a hare, chased it, and failed to catch it because it had disappeared into the garden of some particular old woman, or bolted into her drain. If the huntsmen knocked at her door, they would find her at home, but panting. This went on till one day one of the hounds snapped at the hare's hindquarters as it fled – and when next seen, the old woman was nursing a wounded leg. This story is told of Mother Digby of East Harting, of an unnamed woman at Ditchling, of Dame Garson of Duddleswell, and of four other old women in villages that are not named.

Other transformation tales were less elaborate, but to those who were already inclined to believe them, they seemed quite convincing. For instance, a certain countryman named Tom Reed, whose beliefs and stories (collected ca. 1915) formed the basis of an article in the *Sussex County Magazine* in 1935, declared that a friend of his called Crowhurst once caught an animal in the dark, in the garden of a house alleged to be witch-haunted, but when he called for a light to see what it was that was struggling in his hands, they were empty – 'for you cannot catch a witch', said Reed. Again, Crowhurst once shot a cat in the leg because it would come roaming round the house whenever his wife was out; his wife came home from market limping – 'she had fallen down, so *she* said'.

Or again, another countryman told this tale:

My mates and me was resting under a hedge nigh Up Waltham, 'aving our dinner, when a hare comes lopping along. Darky Tussler says, 'That bain't a hare, that's that —— old 'ooman down along under,' (speaking of a village where we was lodging). I takes up a stone and throws it, and catches that hare. She didn't half holler, letting out a screech just like an ol' 'ooman; an' then she goes limping away. That night, when we was down in village, ol' Sary Weaver, wot people said could make a cow run dry by lookin' at her – folks said she were a witch – comes 'obbling outer 'er cottage. When she sees we, she lets out a screech, same as hare did, an' goes a-limping off, for all the world as if she were that there hare. She were lame in the same leg wot the hare was, but she 'adn't been afore!

The second common Sussex anecdote, about a witch who stopped waggons or carts, was already known 150 years ago. M. A. Lower, writing in 1861, says that in his boyhood he knew of two women reputed to have evil powers; one was said to cause the death of pigs or cattle, and to prevent kettles boiling and butter churning, while the other had the power of stopping any cart that passed her cottage. Lower adds that the lane where she lived was notoriously muddy, which may have been a relevant factor – a commonsense suggestion which may perhaps apply in other cases too, for cottages of impoverished old women are likely to be in the least pleasant parts of a village. Be that as it may, this power was widely believed in. At Ditchling, for instance, stories still circulated in 1935 about an old woman living on the Common some fifty or sixty years previously, who used to halt the carters' waggons as they passed her door:

> The men 'ud beat the hosses, an' they'd pull an' they'd tug, but the waggon wouldn't move, an' the ol' witch 'ud come out a-laughin' an' a-jeerin' at 'em, an' they couldn't get on till she let 'em. But there wor a carter wot knew, an' he guessed he'd be even wid the ol' witch, so he druv he's waggon before her door, an' then it stopped, an' the hosses they tugged, and they pulled, an' they couldn't move it nohow, an' he heard this ol' witch a-laughin' in the cottage. Then this carter what knew, he took out a large knife an' he cuts notches on the spokes, an' there wor a screechin' an' a hollerin' inside, an' out come the ol' witch a-yellin' an' sloppin' blood, an' for every notch on the spokes there wor a cut on her fingers.

The same story is told of a woman at Plumpton; while at Stedham, on the other side of Sussex, there was one who first halted a carter's waggon and then, relenting, herself taught him how to break the spell by flogging the wheel. Up on the Surrey border, the recommended counterspell was to run a knife under each of the horses' hooves, and something similar was done near the Sussex Pad (a pub near swampy land, in North Lancing), according to H. S. Toms:

> I was told at Findon of a witch who resided, not within living memory, in a cottage by the Sussex Pad, near Old Shoreham Bridge; and that when carters passed that way, they were in the habit of running the blade of their pocket-knife round the iron tyres of their waggon-wheels. By some mysterious means, this so affected the witch in her cottage that she was heard to cry aloud in agony.

The motive for such pranks was sometimes revenge; thus,

according to Tom Reed, a certain Old Mother Venus immobilised a carter's horses because he would not run an errand for her, but released them when he gave in. Of another reputed witch (whose name and home were disguised, to spare the feelings of her daughter, still alive in 1943), it was said that the most wicked thing she ever did was to immobilise the Rector's pony and trap all day, not releasing them till eight o'clock in the evening – this was alleged to have happened around 1920!

Witches were also believed to harm farm horses by 'hag-riding' them all night, or by casting the evil eye on them. There were various means to guard against these dangers, such as putting glittering brasses on the harness to deflect the evil, hanging pieces of iron or stones with natural holes in them in the stables, and nailing horseshoes over the door. Even so, horses might still be bewitched. A ploughman had a story about this:

> My ol' man told me that one dark winter mornin' when 'e went into the stable with 'is lantern, 'e finds to 'is amazement the team all with their collars on, an' a-sweatin' an' a-tremblin' fit to drop; one in 'ticular was fair frenzied. So, suspectin' somethin', 'e looks around, an' there on Turpin's back 'e sees two wheat straws, *crossed.* He picks one off, twistin' it, without thinkin' like, an' as 'e did so, tother straw seemed to jump down an' disappear. Then 'e heard a voice, quite distinct, say, 'Come on, Sally, be quick.' An' another voice answered, 'I can't, because me 'eels is tied over me 'ead.' *Bewitched,* they was, 'e said.

Some of these stories may perhaps have a natural explanation at the back of them – some 'hag-ridden' horses, for instance, may have been secretly borrowed by smugglers for their nocturnal journeys. It has been pointed out that a certain Dame Prettylegs, living at Albourne in the nineteenth century, who is said to have been much given to this type of spell, had a husband engaged in smuggling. Even the immobilising of carters' horses could be based on fact; it is known that horses are so sensitive to certain smells that they will refuse to pass an object smeared with the smelly substance, and that ploughman and carters sometimes took advantage of this to play secret tricks on other people – so perhaps some of these alleged witches knew such secrets too.

Similarly, one reputed wizard was obviously simply a man with strong hypnotic power. He was a nineteenth-century farmer known as Pigtail Bridger, 'a very tall, big man, terrible to look at', eccentrically dressed and with his hair in a pigtail. He had the uncanny knack of freezing a man dead in his tracks, and keeping him stuck in the one position while he mocked and jeered at him as long as he chose, the helpless victim being quite conscious all the time. He used to use this means to terrorise and punish the workmen on his farm; for instance, he might lie in wait for one of them as he was coming in to a meal, immobilise him just beside the table, and then himself calmly sit down and eat up the food, taunting the hungry and infuriated man as he did so.

There is an obvious humorous element in several of these anecdotes; as one writer, The Rev H. D. Gordon of Harting, shrewdly noted in 1877:

> Public opinion was lenient with the witch if there was a joke about her story. If, however, fear rather than laughter was appealed to, the 'wise woman' had a hard time of it, and stood in danger of ducking or burning . . . Other humorous lovers of the black arts at Harting had the wonderful power of teasing people in a solemn way – making loads of hay fall off in the streets near quagmires, turning swarms of bees on their creditors and on Sheriff's Officers; and, of course, bewitching small pigs . . . But when witches kill pigs, they become serious . . .

For the most dreaded power of the witch was that of causing sickness, whether in man or beasts. It does not figure so often in the anecdotes, for it does not make such a good story as the witch-hare or the stopped waggon, but there is no doubt that it was taken very seriously indeed. When someone was stricken by any mysterious and stubborn illness, and witchcraft was suspected, the first step was to identify the person concerned, and the second to apply counter-magic. Sometimes 'professional' help was called in, in the person of the 'cunning man' or 'wise woman' who could once be found in almost every country town and village – a person credited with supernatural but benevolent powers, who could provide charms against illness, find lost property, and identify thieves and witches.

Boys Firmin describes one such case in Crowborough in the 1860s. A certain woman was pining away, and no remedy was of any use, until her husband, suspecting witchcraft but not feeling certain of the culprit's identity, consulted a cunning man named Oakley, who lived in Tunbridge Wells. Mr Oakley produced a cupful of some liquid that first fizzed up and then became still and clear; he told the husband to scry in it, and the latter exclaimed excitedly: 'I see her, 'tis Witch Killick! She is the person tormenting my wife!' – Mrs Killick being a neighbour of his, who already had the local reputation of a witch. The cunning man then sent him home with instructions on how to drive off the evil spirit, but what these were is not said.

Alternatively, home-made spells might be used to force the witch to reveal herself and take off the curse. The same Tom Reed mentioned above gave an account of one such procedure, used when the daughter of a friend of his 'wilted and withered' after being given an orange by a woman over the garden gate. Reed thought this counter-magic had saved the girl's life, by forcing the witch to betray her true nature:

> First, the women of the neighbourhood should be informally summoned to the cottage for a chat, or a cup of tea. A cauldron or pot, containing boiling water, must be hanging over the fire, and all the windows, doors and keyholes must be effectually sealed up, under cover of the women's chatter. The tips of the hair or a piece of the fingernail of all those who are present should then be flung into the boiling pot, those of the suspected witch being stealthily taken, as she would be likely to offer resistance. A witch will always scream shrilly when her nails or her hair touch the boiling water, whereas an ordinary mortal will show no sign at all. Should the witch not be of the party, 'witch-noises' are to be expected, outside the window.

Boys Firmin alludes briefly to another form of counter-spell which had to be carried out in complete silence – that is, silence as regards human speech, though 'any amount of noise from heavy hammers and gunpowder was not only permissible but desirable'. But what the spell actually was he does not record.

The well-known counter-spell of the 'witch-bottle' has also been noted in Sussex in the nineteenth century, in connexion with a case of epilepsy. Mrs Latham tells how a friend of hers 'observed, on a cottage hearth, a quart bottle filled with pins, and . . . was requested not to touch the bottle, as it was red-hot, and if she did so, she would spoil the charm'. The woman of the cottage explained that she had consulted a 'wise woman' about her daughter's fits:

> She told me that people afflicted with falling fits were bewitched, and I must get as many pins as would fill a quart bottle, and put them into it, and let it stand close to the fire, upon the hearth, till the pins were red-hot; and, when that came about, they would prick the heart of the witch who had brought this affliction on my poor girl, and she would then be glad enough to take it off.

The effectiveness of the pins would consist not only in their sharpness but also in the fact that they were of iron, a substance universally believed to be powerful against supernatural evil. A red-hot poker was effective too; in Hastings in the 1880s a man whose wife was thought to be bewitched was advised to make her sit by the hearth and to burn her wrists with the poker, 'to make the evil spirit fly up the chimney'. Similarly, one of the Crowborough traditions concerns a woman whose butter refused to 'come', however hard she churned. Suspecting sorcery, her son plunged a red-hot poker into the churn; he heard a loud hiss like a scream, and not long afterwards met Dame Neve, one of the local witches, limping about with a burnt leg. One might also break a witch's spell by scratching her hand 'accidental like', for drawing her blood has long been believed in as a way of destroying her power.

It would be best, of course, never to let her cast a spell at all, but that is easier said than done. For one thing, you must never offend a witch; for another, you must never eat or drink in her presence; for a third, you must not accept anything she tries to give you, for instance money – one man who simply agreed to do a witch's shopping for her and took her money from her to pay for it, was said to have fallen ill in consequence. In short, the only safe thing was to have nothing to do with her at all. In order to know who was and who was not a witch, it was useful to own a spayed bitch, for they could invariably detect them. The witches themselves, it was thought, could always recognise one another:

> When two witches meet on the road, they don't speak, and they don't stop, and they don't even nod at each other, however

much they may be friends; they just laugh softly, and pass on.

Another recurrent feature in the Sussex traditions was the belief that a witch could not die while still in possession of her powers and secrets, and still attended by her familiars. Boys Firmin describes how in Crowborough people said that no witch could die till someone came to her bed to receive her 'spirit' from her, but the longer she lived, the worse it was for her, since the spirit, which was inside her body, tormented her more and more. For this reason, when Witch Killick was dying in the 1860s, her daughter was persuaded, much against her will, to come to her bedside and receive her mother's 'spirit' into her own body, so that the old woman might die. The same belief is shown in Tom Reed's account of the death of 'Old Mother Venus', at which his own mother had been present. The old woman's last act was to pass her hand rapidly across the bosom of one of the women at her bedside, after which she fell back dead. The younger woman denied having been given anything, but from that day her cottage was haunted in poltergeist fashion, and soon she left home and moved to Kent; Reed believed she had been given a mouse.

The belief is certainly old. In Hurstpierpoint in 1895 there were memories of a certain Nanny Smart who had lived there a hundred years before, and was much feared for her ability to put people in a trance and to immobilise horses. It was said that 'she could not die unless someone bought the secrets of her life, and at last a man from Cuckfield bought them for a halfpenny, and she died in a blue flame'. The man, whose name was Old Hockland, died in Hurstpierpoint workhouse in the 1830s.

There is a strong similarity between these various anecdotes about Sussex witches in the last hundred and fifty years or so, so that we obviously see here recurrent story-patterns which become attached to particular individuals to whom they seem appropriate, in just the same way as recurrent tales of treasures or underground passages are attached to appropriate features in the countryside. It would be very interesting, both psychologically and sociologically, to know more about the women who became the focus for this lore – what it was about them that attracted it in the first place, and how they themselves reacted to their reputation. The material is too scanty for proper analysis, but the picture that emerged would, I suspect, be an unhappy one.

The Rev Thomas Geering, writing about Hailsham in the late

nineteenth century, noted that all the reputed witches he had ever known or heard of had been poor; he describes one whom he himself had feared as a boy – decrepit, housebound, poor, and shunned by all the children, who believed that she used her walking-stick to ride to the moon 'on nightly errands of mischief'. She knew of the rumours about her, and used to say: 'If I *was* a witch, I would never want for snuff.' A more recent writer describes how, in an unnamed village, gangs of boys used to follow an alleged witch round the streets on sunny days, with open pocket-knives in their hands; they thought that if they could stick a knife in her shadow she would have to stand still, or might even fall down, but she always heard them and looked round, at which they ran away. A minor matter, no doubt, not to be compared with real ostracism, but unpleasant all the same.

On the other hand, there is some evidence that some alleged witches exploited their reputation to their own advantage. It is said of old Nanny Smart in eighteenth-century Hurstpierpoint that she 'would go into anyone's house and have tea with them' because they were too frightened of her to wish to annoy her, and of an old and crippled witch in Hastings in 1830 that 'she seemed to delight that she, old and miserable as she was, could keep in awe so many happier and stronger fellow-creatures'. Of yet another, who flourished as late as the 1890s, it was said:

> Her reputation was very valuable to her. If she stopped a child and said, 'What a fine crop of plums your mother had down in Crabtree Lane, dearie,' the result would be a basket of the best plums, as otherwise the tree would wither and die. So she kept herself provided with good things.

But on balance, the reputed witch's situation must have been an unhappy one, if only because the belief that it was dangerous to accept anything from her hand or to eat in her presence must have isolated her from normal social contacts, while an atmosphere of fear, suspicion and hatred surrounded her. How cruel such isolation could be when the woman suspected was old and ailing comes out clearly in a description published in the *Sussex County Magazine* in 1943 – the events described having occurred as recently as 1920, or thereabouts:

> That kind of wicked old woman always has books – powerful

books, which have a deal of evil written in them. I know Betsey had books, because I've seen them.

She was a very old woman at the time I'm telling you of, and when her husband – a quiet, ordinary chap – died, she found it hard to carry on as she'd been used to. For one thing, money was short, and for another thing her wickedness was rewarded with chronic rheumatics. She went on as best she could, but it was not easy, as no one would lend her a hand, being frightened of what she might do to them. She used to swear away to herself when she lifted potatoes from the garden, and made a great trouble of going to the farm for milk. I remember the farmer wouldn't let her pass the gate for fear she would put a spell on the cows. She had to get on the road side of the gate and holler out. The farmer's wife were a bit hard of hearing, and many's the time old Betsey stood there and bawled her head off for half an hour at a time. Then her rheumaticky hands made it hard for her to do a bit of washing on a Monday morning.

Gradually she dropped off coming into the village for provisions, making one visit do a long time, until one day the farmer said in the Woodman's Arms that old Betsey must be drinking ale, as she hadn't been near him for milk for quite a week . . . Well, to cut a long story short, the keeper did tell the Rector, who called at the old woman's cottage that afternoon to find her ill in bed, hardly able to move a finger.

The workhouse people came next day and took her away. One of the head men stayed behind to sort out her belongings. She hadn't much furniture, but they found a pile of books. My neighbour, who was very fond of reading and very curious as well, asked the official if he could have them, or at least read them, but we said it wasn't right, and anyway we didn't want anyone else learning the secrets and playing us up – Betsey Shadlow was trouble enough – and we asked the workhouse chap to burn them. He looked at them, and said they were rubbish anyway.

It's a strange thing, but when they came to set fire to all the unwanted stuff from the cottage along with those books, we lookers-on saw *green* flames coming from the fire!

8 Healing Charms and Magic Cures

THE SUBJECT OF FOLK MEDICINE is extensive, covering a wide range of cures from the purely practical to the frankly magical, and he would be a bold man who would undertake to say with complete certainty, when faced with some of the old country recipes, precisely where medicine ends and magic begins. For instance, several Sussex writers say that the fat of an adder, melted down into oil, was highly prized as a cure for deafness; indeed, one man is said to have regularly sold it to a chemist in Uckfield at a guinea an ounce, late in the nineteenth century. It is a fact that oil will soothe ear-ache and loosen wax in the ears, but the particular value placed on adder's oil may well have been due to the mistaken notion that adders are deaf, and if so the principle involved is no longer medical but magical – the idea that like cures like.

Similarly, wrapping flannel round the affected part is obviously a sensible treatment for rheumatism, bronchitis, and sore throats, all of which are relieved by warmth; but to insist that the flannel must be red verges on the magical (red as a symbol of heat or of blood is presumably the underlying idea), and one is definitely over the borderline with such recipes as a skein of red silk round the waist to prevent lumbago, or a strip of red flannel folded seven times and drawn between the toes to prevent cramp in the feet – both of which were still current in the 1920s. In this chapter I shall not attempt to cover the many herbal cures and similar examples of old-fashioned practical country medicine, but will concentrate on those where some form of magical principle or procedure is involved.

The clearest cases are those where the cure is performed by virtue of some secret supernatural power believed to reside in particular people, the 'charmers', 'wise women' and 'cunning men' who played an important role in the old village communities. Several incidents quoted in the previous chapter showed how these were consulted in cases where witchcraft was suspected, but they were also often sought out in less dramatic circumstances. In Fittleworth, at the time when Mrs Latham was collecting folklore there, there were several women who performed cures by reciting certain charms, or, as they preferred to call them, 'blessings'. One was for the healing of wounds caused by thorns:

> Our Saviour Christ was of a pure Virgin born,
> And He was crownèd with a thorn.
> I hope it may not rage or swell;
> I trust in God it may do well.

Another, for curing burns and scalds, could only be performed on a Sunday evening; Mrs Latham knew of a case where a scalded woman refused all medical help and insisted on waiting, in great pain, till the Sunday came round, when she sent for the charmer. The latter bowed her head, crossed two fingers over the burn, murmured some words to herself, and blew on the burn, whereupon the woman declared herself cured. The words were:

> There came two Angels from the north;
> One was Fire, and one was Frost.
> Out, Fire; in, Frost,
> **In the name of Father, Son and Holy Ghost.**

The 'wise women' Mrs Latham met regarded their knowledge of such 'blessings' as a precious privilege by which they could help their neighbours, and would make no charge for using them. Similarly, in Lewes in the 1880s, there was a certain Janet Steer who kept a shop in Malling Street, and who was known as a 'wise woman' who could cure warts. Her method was to count the warts and then buy them from the patient for a halfpenny. People thought that she believed that if she sold her wisdom she would no longer prosper, and that that was why she used a method which left her financially the loser. Probably, to judge by similar cases in other parts of England, charmers who held such views might be tactfully thanked for their services by a gift of food or some other payment in kind, after a discreet lapse of time.

'Professional' healers of this type were still in practice in quite recent times. In 1939, Dr P. H. Lulham wrote in the *Sussex County Magazine* that a few years previously, during an outbreak of diphtheria, he had found out that some mothers were taking their children to a local 'wise woman'. She would first tie a hazel twig round their throats, for which she charged a shilling, and then, if that failed, she would make them swallow a bit of stewed mouse while she recited an incantation, for which she charged half-a-crown. The doctor got the police to put a stop to her cures; what incantation she used he did not record. Indeed, it would not be surprising if a few charmers were still to be found quietly practising their ancient craft, for instance as healers of warts; certainly the memory of those who flourished a generation or two ago must still be very fresh.

But it was not only these 'professional' healers who were credited with mysterious powers; certain specific cures could be performed by people who were peculiar in one particular respect, whatever their normal station in life. According to one of Mrs Latham's informants, thrush, a disease of the mouth and throat in children, could be cured if a 'left twin' were to blow three times into the sick child's mouth – a 'left twin' being one of a pair of which the other had died. If the sick child was a boy, the 'left twin' had to be a female, and vice versa. According to a later writer, the blowing had to be done by someone who had been born as a posthumous child, and must be repeated three days running, the patient being fasting at the time. In both cases, the healer's peculiarity is that he has survived the death of someone very closely linked with him; perhaps he was imagined to be

F

endowed with a double portion of 'the breath of life' in consequence.

Even more macabre was a remedy for goitre or for a wen on the throat – the touch of a dead man's hand on the affected part. The explanation lies in an older form of the charm, which required the touch to be that of a hanged man's hand as he swung on the gibbet. Mrs Latham describes how her childhood walks on Beeding Hill in the 1840s were spoilt by her terror of an ancient gibbet which stood there, and by the gruesome tales concerning it which her nurse insisted on relating. One of these was about a woman who was cured of a wen on her neck by the touch of a dead murderer's hand – 'she was taken under the gallows in a cart and was held up in order that she might touch the dead hand, and she passed it three times over the wen, and then returned homewards'. The nurse was not romancing; there is a description of just such a scene at a public execution in the *Brighton Herald* in 1835. With the cessation of public hangings this gruesome procedure became impossible, and the appropriate magical symbolism whereby a hanged man was used to cure afflictions of the neck was extended to corpses of any sort.

In other cases, it is hard to see any appropriateness in the peculiarity which confers a power to heal certain diseases. Whooping cough, it was once thought, could be cured by any remedy whatsoever which happened to be recommended by a man riding a piebald horse. Mrs Latham knew a man who had such a horse, and who was constantly being asked to suggest remedies; he would answer quite arbitrarily, and his advice was always taken. Another cure for the same trouble, recorded in 1931, was to feed the sufferer on bread and butter given by a family where the head of the household was called John, and his wife Joan. At Ringmer in the early nineteenth century, convulsions were thought to be cured by wearing a silver ring bought with six sixpences, each coin having been donated by a bachelor; it was important that the donors should not be thanked.

Certain charms did not require the intervention of a healer, but were administered by the sufferer himself. There was one against toothache which was thought to be so powerful that simply to have it written in one's Bible or Prayer Book was enough, or so Mrs Latham was told by an old man who showed her his copy:

As Peter sat weeping on a marvel [?marble] stone, Christ

came by and said unto him, 'Peter, what ailest thou?' Peter answered and said unto him, 'My Lord and my God, my tooth acheth.' Jesus said unto him, 'Arise, Peter, and be thou whole; and not thou only but all them that carry these lines for my sake shall never have the toothache.'

It will be noticed that this charm describes a miracle worked by Christ on St Peter – an episode which does not, of course, figure in any of the Gospels. Allusions to real or alleged incidents in the lives of Christ or the saints are quite frequent in charms, and gave them a religious status in the minds of those who used them; the charm for thorn wounds quoted above is of this type, and that for burns mentions angels who on some mysterious past occasion 'came from the north'. The structure of such charms is very like that of many orthodox prayers which recall some Divine Act from the past in order to pray for a comparable grace in the present. Not surprisingly, therefore, the country people often called such formulae 'blessings' rather than 'charms'.

Another self-administered charm with an element of prayer in it is that recorded by the Rev W. D. Parish, against ague:

> Ague, ague, I thee defy!
> Three days shiver,
> Three days shake;
> Make me well for Jesus' sake.

There is an element of realistic prognosis here; ague is normally an intermittent disease, which may well clear up of its own accord after a few days, but the patient also assisted nature by the magical procedure of writing the charm on a three-cornered piece of paper and wearing it round his neck till it dropped off. Three, always a potent number, here probably more particularly symbolises the three days of shivering and shaking, though it might also be intended to invoke the Trinity, often symbolised by a triangle.

A different, and purely magical, principle is involved in another ague charm which one Sussex writer's nurse had seen in use in her own childhood (presumably towards the end of the nineteenth century): she had seen a man unwinding lengths of rope which he had coiled round his body onto a tree, as he ran round and round its trunk, singing:

> Ague, ague, I thee defy;
> Ague, ague, to this tree I thee tie.

This is a clear case of transference magic; the disease was being ritually 'given' to the tree. The nurse who had seen this done firmly believed that one could indeed rid oneself of sickness by this method, or by standing in a pond, 'if you knew the way'. Another writer records a different method of transferring ague to a tree, in this case specifically stated to be an aspen – an appropriate choice, since its leaves shiver in the lightest breeze. You must take clippings from the sufferer's finger- and toe-nails while he is asleep, without his knowing (a difficult condition!), and also cut some hair from the nape of his neck; you must wrap them in paper and put them in a hole in an aspen tree.

One well-known ague cure involved the use of a spider. Some said it should be swallowed alive, rolled in its own web, on an empty stomach; others, that it should be put in a bag with a few flies to keep it alive, and worn round the neck till 'one of these days you'll find the ague has gone'. The lapse of time makes this a safe prophecy, but why a spider? I would hazard the guess that this is once again a matter of like curing like; the shivers of an ague bout, so vividly described in the Sussex saying 'Old Johnny's running his finger down my back', find a parallel in the shivers one feels when a spider runs over one's flesh, so that the latter might be thought a good counter-irritant to cure the former.

Symbolical appropriateness probably lies behind several other curious cures, though the point is not explicitly made in any of the sources. The use of adder's oil for deafness is one that has already been mentioned; others are to carry a mole's paw against rheumatism, cramp or toothache (moles are strong diggers, and will gnaw roots that are in their way); to make children with teething troubles eat rabbits' brains or wear a baked shrew in a bag round their necks (both animals have sharp teeth); to give powdered human skull for epilepsy (a brain disease), or marrow and oil extracted from human bones for rheumatism (presumably the type which affects bones rather than muscles). On the other hand, there are many recipes which cannot be explained by this principle: take woodlice in wine for dropsy; eat boiled whelps and worms for gunshot wounds; grasp horseradish scrapings for headache; carry a potato in your pocket against rheumatism; swallow a live frog to cure or prevent tuberculosis; or go among a flock of sheep for the same complaint, as a shepherd recommended as late as 1936:

> They do say that if people with consumption walk about among the sheep in the morning when they are leaving the fold, it will do them a power of good. Sheep have a funny smell – not a nasty one, but a very healthy one, and they say that that is what does the consumptives good.

Nor can one see any reason why mice should be a highly popular prescription for all sorts of ailments, apart from the practical fact that they are easily obtainable, and apparently quite palatable – tasting rather like chicken. They had many uses: cooked with onions, they would cure whooping-cough; baked to a cinder, powdered, and mixed with jam, they would cure a child of bed-wetting; dried and powdered they were good for diabetes; while to eat one roasted followed by two powdered was another recipe against whooping-cough. They were such a standard feature of folk medicine that there was a joke current at one time about a doctor who was treating a young child with a high fever, who told the mother to put some mice in a bag on the child's forehead; next day she reported gratefully, 'He's much better now, sir; the fever has gone down, and the mice are dead.'

This woman – if the joke is based on a real incident, which is quite possible – clearly believed in the transference of disease to an animal by contact. There is an undoubted instance of this in a cure for goitre briefly mentioned by the Rev J. Coker Egerton in 1884, and described in more detail by Miss L. N. Candlin as having been in use at Withyham 'less than a hundred years ago'. It is to take a live snake and draw it nine times round the goitre, then to cork it up in a bottle and bury it deep in the ground; as it dried and shrivelled, so the goitre would disappear. Similarly, one might rub a snail on a wart and then impale it on a thorn; as the snail shrivelled, so the wart would shrink.

Another type of magic cure depends on the opposite principle: that a living object, in these cases a growing plant, can transfer something of its 'life force' to those who come in contact with it. One dramatic example was recorded by the Rev Henry Hoper, Rector of Portslade from 1815 to 1859, who found that only a few years before his time his parishioners used to believe that 'a dying person will recover if carried round thrice and thrice bumped against a thorn tree of great antiquity on the Downs, ever ready to dispense its magic power to all believers'; the procedure had actually been tried not long before, but to everyone's surprise it had failed. Later in the nineteenth century, Mrs Latham noted a widespread belief that the maple tree confers long life on any child that is passed between its branches; there was one in West Grinstead Park in her time, and she observed that much distress was caused by a rumour that it was to be cut down. Probably also to be classed here is the belief that one can cure oneself of fits (or, some say, of boils) by crawling three times through the arch formed by a bramble shoot which has curled over and re-rooted itself at the tip.

The most elaborate and interesting procedure of this type is one for curing a child of a hernia. The tree chosen for the ritual, the ash, is one that is regarded as having protective magic qualities (for instance, against snakes, witches, and evil spirits); the splitting of the tree imitates the rupture from which the child is suffering, and hence its healing is designed, according to the principle of imitative magic, to promote the child's; magic numbers are prominent; the act of passing the child through the tree may possibly mimic childbirth; and a permanent magical connexion is set up between the child's life and the tree's. All these points emerge from Mrs Latham's full account:

A child so afflicted must be passed nine times every morning on nine successive days at sunrise through a cleft in a sapling ash-tree, which has been so far given up by the owner of it to the parents of the child as that there is an understanding that it shall not be cut down during the life of the infant that is to be passed through it. The sapling must be sound at heart, and the cleft must be made with an axe. The child, on being carried to the tree, must be attended by nine persons, each of whom must pass it through the cleft from west to east. On the ninth morning the solemn ceremony is concluded by binding the tree tightly with a cord, and it is supposed that as the cleft closes the health of the child will improve. In the neighbourhood of Petworth some cleft ashes may be seen, through which children have very recently [i.e. in the 1870s] been passed. I may add that only a few weeks since, a person who had lately purchased an ash-tree standing in this parish [Fittleworth], intending to cut it down, was told by the father of a child who had some time before been passed through it, that the infirmity would be sure to return upon his son if it were felled. Whereupon the good man said, he knew such would be the case; and therefore he would not fell it for the world.

Such beliefs in the magical powers of trees are probably now quite extinct, but belief in the protection afforded by stones with a natural hole in them lingered into more recent times; within living memory such stones, sometimes draped with a red cloth or tied with red ribbon, were hung over people's beds to keep nightmares away. In its origins this practice really belongs more with the use of protective amulets against witchcraft and evil spirits, for there was a time when nightmares were believed to be caused by 'hag-riding'; however, Sussex sources in the last century or so do not seem to make any connexion between witches and nightmares, so that the practice may appropriately be included here. Cecile Woodford has recently described how her grandmother, a midwife and healer, used to use holed stones to 'scrape diseases off children' and to prevent adults catching them.

The range of magical folk-medicine reported by Sussex writers is wide and varied, but is certainly by no means a complete survey of what must have existed. It will be noticed, for instance, that nothing has been said about any aspect of midwifery, nor about any of the more unpleasant or embarrassing diseases. This is certainly due to the nature of the sources, namely books and articles designed for the general public in a comparatively reticent age, and probably also to the social standing of their authors, who were unlikely to be told anything 'not nice' by their informants. Mrs Latham, herself a clergyman's wife, mentions her hesitation at including in her very valuable discussion of Sussex folk-medicine two cures for bed-wetting. Fortunately, she overcame her distaste, for one of the procedures is a most striking application of the paradoxical principle (already exemplified in the case of gibbet-corpses and 'left twins') that contact with death can be a curative force, while the other involves another use of the beneficent ash-tree. Moreover, both display an interesting use of psychology; the traumatic experience of being made to defile such sacred spots as a grave and the domestic hearth might well have a powerful effect on the unfortunate child, though whether the shock would be entirely beneficial is perhaps doubtful:

When a poor child has in vain been whipped and scolded for the nightly repetition of a certain involuntary offence, in the last resort one of the following remedies may be tried. Upon the day appointed for the funeral of a person not of the same sex as the child, while the first part of the burial service is being read within the church, the child is to be taken to the open grave, and is there to do that which constituted the original offence. My informant told me that, although she had taken her own little boy to the churchyard, he had not the courage to carry out the first remedy, so she tried the second, with complete success. It consists in the child's first going alone to fix upon an ash-tree suitable for the purposes of the charm, and going afterwards upon another day, without divulging its intention, to gather a handful of the ash-keys, which it must lay with the left hand in the hollow of the right arm. Thus are they to be carried home, and then they are to be burned to ashes. The charm is then completed by the child performing the same ceremony over the embers on the hearth, which in the former remedy it was to go through at the open grave.

9 From the Cradle to the Grave

THE GREAT TURNING-POINTS OF LIFE – birth, marriage, death – are inevitably marked by ceremonies both religious and secular, and inevitably, too, are surrounded by various traditional beliefs and customs. Yet, as so often, it can be difficult to tell whether a custom does or does not contain elements of irrationality; when for instance, somebody seeing a friend's young baby for the first time slips a silver coin into its hand (as is still commonly done), is this mere present-giving? Or is it meant to ensure luck, and particularly wealth, for the baby's later life? The latter seems likelier, and the principle involved would then be 'begin as you mean to go on'.

One custom which certainly embodies this principle was noted by Mrs Latham in the 1860s, and was indeed still current, according to another Sussex writer, in the 1940s: in order that a new-born baby should thrive well, it is vital that when he is to be moved for the first time from the room in which he was born, he should be carried upstairs before he is carried down. If this is impossible, because he was born in a top-floor room, some other way of raising him must be found – for instance, someone holding him might climb onto a step-ladder or a tall piece of furniture, and this would be enough to break the bad luck. The implied magical symbolism is of course that of healthy upward growth contrasted with a downward, graveward, movement.

The idea of lucky days and hours has not had as much influence as one might expect on beliefs about birth. Almost the only trace of it is an old notion, now obsolete, that children born on a Sunday or on Christmas Day would never be drowned or hanged; the nursery rhyme beginning 'Monday's child is fair of face', which is known in Sussex as elsewhere; and a former belief that those born on the stroke of midnight would grow up able to see ghosts. To these fragments of old rural lore may be added, in modern times, a widespread semi-serious belief in astrology fostered by newspapers and commercial interests, and the associated taste for 'lucky birthstones'.

Warding off evil spirits from a new-born baby must once have been an important branch of the midwife's art, but I have only come across one reference to it : Cecile Woodford tells how her grandmother, a Newhaven midwife, used to brush the baby's face with a rabbit's foot for this purpose.

Sacraments and religious ceremonies were formerly sometimes valued for rather unorthodox reasons, in particular for their supposed good effect on one's health. One of Mrs Latham's informants, who was clearly suffering from post-natal depression, said to her : 'I feel very weak and teary after my confinement, but I daresay I shall get up my strength after I have been churched.' There also lingered some confused memory of the archaic notion that a woman was 'unclean' after childbirth until she had been churched, and that her behaviour during this period must be governed by various taboos; this is seen in the belief that it is dangerous for a woman to carry her baby across running water if she has not been churched, which was occasionally to be found two generations ago.

Baptism was similarly regarded as health-giving, and possibly still is; fretful or ailing babies, it was thought, would be helped by it. Various superstitions surrounded this sacrament; it was held to be unlucky to reveal the chosen name to outsiders before the ceremony, or to wipe off the baptismal water from the child's head. But the most vital point – and one which is still sometimes noted and commented on – was that the baby must cry during the ceremony, and that this proves that the Devil has left it. Among Roman Catholics, it is said that it ought to cry at the moment when salt is put on its tongue (not surprisingly, it often does); among Anglicans and Nonconformists, who use no salt, the precise moment is not specified. Mrs Latham remarked on the prevalence of this belief in her time, 'even among the educated classes' :

> I was lately present at a christening in Sussex, when a lady of the party, who was grandmother of the child, whispered in a voice of anxiety, 'The child never cried; why did the nurse not rouse it up?' After we had left church she said to her, 'Oh, Nurse, why did you not pinch baby?' And when the baby's good behaviour was afterwards commented upon, she observed, with a serious air, 'I wish that he had cried.'

There were also a few taboos relating to the care of young children. If you cut a baby's nails before he is one year old, he will grow up to be a thief, so you must only trim them by biting them short. And when the child begins to lose his milk teeth, you must never throw them away, for if an animal should find one and gnaw it the corresponding tooth in the child's new set will grow deformed, resembling that of the animal in question. The informant who told Mrs Latham about this in the 1860s knew an old man who had one huge tooth shaped like a pig's tusk, who blamed it on his mother's stupidity in throwing one of his milk teeth in the trough. Finally, it may be noted that to rock an empty cradle was regarded as a sure way to bring about the birth of more babies, though whether this was looked on as good or bad luck depended on circumstances.

> If you rock the cradle empty,
> Then you shall have babies plenty.

A natural preoccupation of young people with love and marriage inspired various rituals (mostly performed by girls) intended to reveal whom one was fated to marry, or whether an existing romance would develop favourably. The most interesting of these are the seasonal ones associated with the January New Moon, Midsummer Eve, and Hallowe'en, which will be described in the next chapter. There were also ways of telling the future from cards, tea-leaves, apple-peel, or cherry-stones; these, however, are practically universal in England and still well known, so they need no description here.

More characteristic of the countryside is the picturesque saying, 'When the gorse is not in bloom, then kissing's not in fashion' — the point being that gorse blooms all the year round, even if the blossoms are few at certain seasons. Equally pleasant was the Sussex custom that young men, when they went out courting, used to carry a 'honeysuckle stick' to bring them luck and to indicate their intentions. Such a stick is one cut from the stem of a tree (preferably hazel) which has been distorted by a honey-suckle growing up it, so that it is marked by a deep, twisting groove and a corresponding ridge of swollen bark. In popular songs and verses, a clinging honeysuckle often symbolises a woman's faithful love; hence it brings good luck to lovers.

In some villages, a curious taboo was current in the nineteenth century: a man should not attend the church services at which his own banns were called — 'hearing hisself church-bawled', as dialect speakers put it — for if he did, his first child would be born deaf, or even deaf and dumb. Weddings themselves, of course, are a focus for many picturesque customs, often intended to bring luck and fertility. One charming one, common in the nineteenth century, was strewing the path outside the church as the couple emerged. The strewers were often poor women with babies in their arms, and would expect a tip for their pains; they threw flowers, wheat, and sometimes sugar plums. The bride's wreath and posy sometimes included an ear of wheat and a twig of gorse. Next morning, the happy pair might also find that the threshold of their home had been strewn with flowers in the night. More-over, families following certain trades had their own ways of celebrating weddings; fishermen trimmed their boats with flowers and ribbons, and millers set the mill-sails in the position known as 'The Miller's Glory', i.e. like a St George's, not a St Andrew's, Cross.

But not all weddings lead to happy marriages. Lower, describing bridal strewing in 1861, adds that a very different type of strewing could occur. When a man was known to beat his wife too much, the neighbours might express their disapproval by emptying a bag of straw and chaff at his door, punning on the words 'threshing' and 'thrashing'. This is a typical example of the ritual ways in which rural communities expressed contempt and disapproval, usually for offenders against the decencies of family life. Another was the hanging in effigy once practised at Horsham on St Crispin's Day (see below, pp 132–3). Another was 'Rough Music', which consisted in visiting the offender's home after dark, sometimes for several nights running, and serenading him or her by clashing tongs and pots and pans, booing and yelling, rattling bones, blowing cow-horns, and so forth. Three instances at East Lavant between 1869 and 1872 were typical; two were against men who bullied their wives, the third against a woman who beat her husband. Such demonstrations were often a form of intimidation intended to drive the victim out of the village.

Like many old customs, Rough Music may reappear unexpectedly in our own times, if feelings run high, as can be seen from the following account, given by a schoolmistress, of the reaction to an alleged case of cruelty to a child in about 1950:

About seven years ago, Rough Music was made for a certain family at Copthorne, in Sussex. One Saturday night, about 11 p.m., I heard the sound of shouting and banging on metal coming from about half a mile from where I then lived. I did not know what it was all about at the time, but soon afterwards I heard that the family in question were being shunned by the villagers, and demonstrations made against them. The reason for this was that the father had smacked the little boy next door for hitting his own little girl with a brick. The boy developed pneumonia shortly afterwards, and his mother claimed that it was the result of the man's blow. There was a court case about it, but it was dismissed.

However, the villagers were determined to have their 'pound of flesh', and started 'rough musicking' the family. I only heard it once myself, but I understand that the demonstration was repeated on several successive Saturday nights. There was a procession and the traditional noise on each occasion, but no effigy was carried. The victims tried to stick it out, but it was too much for them in the end, and eventually they sold their cottage and moved from the district.

The men of Copthorne took to violence after having tried and failed to get redress at law. Dissatisfaction with the law accounts for the growth of other surprising pseudo-legal ceremonies which uneducated people in former centuries performed publicly, in the conviction that they were legally binding. One of these, the 'Smock Wedding', was believed to be a way of circumventing an unpopular law concerning the remarriage of widows whose husbands had died in debt, which decreed that their second husbands would become liable for the debts. The bawdy aspect of 'Smock Weddings' tickled the humour of eighteenth-century journalists, so that the *Sussex Weekly Advertiser* printed two accounts of such incidents, in March 1770 and November 1794:

> Last Monday a maltster in this town [Lewes] was married to a widow whose husband died enthralled [i.e. heavily in debt]; he, to save himself the obligation of paying her late husband's debts, took her in her smock only, she going across the street to his appartments with no one thing on her but her shift, which was witnessed by Cork Fig.

> On Tuesday last, Mr. F. Hollingdale, of Barcombe, was married to a widow of the same place named Ford. In order to get rid of some pecuniary obligations, it was judged expedient by the above couple that the bride should cross the High Road, attired in a chemise only, in the presence of three male witnesses. Three neighbours were accordingly sent for, without being informed of the occasion, before whom the widow performed the curious ceremony; but as one of the witnesses was so confounded by what he saw as to render him incapable of swearing to particulars, 'tis doubted whether the stratagem of the newly-married pair will prove successful.

Just as dissatisfaction with the laws of debt fostered this remarkable pseudo-legal procedure, so the difficulty of obtaining divorce until this century gave rise to the formal 'selling' of wives, well-known to readers of Thomas Hardy's novel, *The Mayor of Casterbridge*. For the rich, of course, divorce had long been available; but for the working classes the slow, expensive legalities were a daunting obstacle. In the eighteenth and nineteenth centuries, however, many of them firmly believed that a woman was her husband's legal property, and that he could get rid of her by selling her, provided this was publicly done and certain formalities observed; usually she would be handed over to her new owner with a halter round her neck, always before witnesses, and sometimes with a 'legal' document to confirm the transaction.

That invaluable repository of scandal, the *Sussex Weekly Advertiser*, describes several cases: at Ninfield in November 1790 a man sold his wife one evening for half a pint of gin, duly handed her over next morning in a halter, but later changed his mind and bought her back 'at an advanced price'; at Lewes in July 1797 a blacksmith sold his wife to one of his journeymen 'agreeably to an engagement drawn up by an attorney for that purpose'; while at Brighton in February 1799 a man named Staines 'sold his wife by private contract, for 5s and eight pots of beer, to one James Marten of the same place', with two married couples witnessing 'the articles of separation and sale'.

The custom persisted into the nineteenth century. Harry Burstow mentions three cases in his *Reminiscences of Horsham*:

I have been told of a woman named Smart who, about 1820, was sold at Horsham for 3s and 6d. She was bought by a man named Steere, and lived with him at Billingshurst. She had two children by each of these husbands. Steere afterwards discovered that Smart had parted with her because she had qualities which he could endure no longer, and Steere, discovering the same qualities himself, sold her to a man named Greenfield, who endured, or never discovered, or differently valued the said qualities till he died.

Again, at the November Fair, 1825, a journeyman blacksmith, whose name I never learned, with the greatest effrontery exhibited for sale his wife, with a halter round her neck. She was a good-looking woman with three children, and was actually sold for £2 5s, the purchaser agreeing to take one of the children. This 'deal' gave offence to some who were present, and they reported the case to the magistrate, but the contracting parties, presumably satisfied, quickly disappeared, and I never heard any more about them.

The last case happened about 1844, when Ann Holland, known as 'pin-toe Nanny' or 'Nanny pin-toe', was sold for £1 10s. Nanny was led into the market place with a halter round her neck. Many people hissed and booed, but the majority took the matter good-humouredly. She was 'knocked down' to a man named Johnson, at Shipley, who sold his watch to buy her for the above sum. This bargain was celebrated on the spot by the consumption of a lot of beer by Nanny, her new husband, and friends. She lived with Johnson for one year, during which she had one child, then ran away – finally marrying a man named Jim Smith, with whom she apparently lived happy for many years.

Nanny may have been the last woman sold at Horsham, but an editorial note in the *Sussex County Magazine* for 1926 asserts that the practice survived elsewhere to the very end of the last century:

> As late as 1898 the old belief that it was quite legal for a man to sell his wife had not quite died out, for the newspapers of that day reported that at the end of the harvest at Yapton, near Littlehampton, a man 'sold his wife to a stranger for 3s'.

The darker aspects of life, sickness and the approach of death, naturally figure largely in any account of everyday superstitions. Magical 'cures' for illness have been discussed already, but there remains the extensive lore of death omens, once commonly observed, and very likely still not forgotten entirely. Some are drawn from funerals and other circumstances surrounding a death, and were held to mean that a second death would follow shortly: a corpse that fails to stiffen normally, a heavy note in the passing bell, a rattling church door, an unexpected encounter with a funeral procession – all these forebode death. Moreover, 'deaths go in threes'. Or the link with death may be symbolical, as with dull fires which will not burn up, coffin-shaped creases in sheets, or dreams of fallen trees.

Other omens were drawn from animal behaviour and cries: persistently howling dogs, croaking ravens or carrion-crows, the screech-owl's shriek, the knocking of the death-watch beetle, bees swarming on a dead branch. Birds were particularly feared; even in the 1930s a bird flying into a room might still be thought a death omen, or if (as happened at Amberley at this period) unusual numbers of robins were seen around a cottage, the phenomenon was later interpreted as having foretold the deaths of the owner and his wife. A bird and a specified person may be linked; the death of a Bishop of Chichester is always foretold, they say, by the arrival of a heron which perches on the cathedral spire.

Flowers might be ill-omened too. It would be 'bringing death into the house' to bring in hawthorn blossoms, white lilac, or the flower of the broom, at any rate in May. There used also to be a fear of snowdrops and primroses if it was only a single blossom, not a whole bunch, that was picked. Both were probably associated with death because they were formerly often strewn on coffins and planted in graveyards; also, as one woman told Mrs Latham, a snowdrop 'looks like a corpse in its shroud, and grows so near the ground'.

Mrs Latham also came upon a widespread belief in the appearance of 'corpse-lights', small faint lights flitting near the houses of people fated soon to die; in her view, they were simply glow-worms. One of her informants believed that deaths were heralded by the sight of some mysterious animal of supernatural whiteness; her own argument that the creature was merely a white cat did not at all convince the speaker.

When a sick man was at the point of death, certain rituals could ease his passing. Doors and windows should be opened, to let the soul leave freely; if he still lingered, some would open drawers and cupboards too. It was often held that if there were game-birds' or pigeons' feathers on the pillows or bed, the dying man would remain in agony. A nurse once told Mrs Latham how she was alone in a house with an old man who was 'dying hard'; he was too heavy for her to lift him and pull the feather bed from under him, so she tied a rope round his waist and hauled him bodily onto the floor, where 'he went off in a minute quite comfortable, just like a lamb'.

The funeral customs of Sussex present few unusual features. There are some slight traces of an old belief that to put salt on coffins afforded them protection against evil forces; one writer mentions an old woman's recollection that a High Church priest, some time in the late nineteenth century, offended people in her village by forbidding them to sprinkle coffins with salt 'to stop the Devil flying off with the body'. More frequently mentioned is a charming custom at the burial of shepherds; a lock of wool was laid in their hands in the coffin, so that at the Last Day they could prove what their work had been, and so be forgiven for the many times they had had to miss Sunday church. The custom was sometimes kept up in this century, for instance at Alfriston and Falmer in the 1930s; in the latter village, a shepherd was buried with crook, shears and sheep-bell at his side.

G

Alfriston also once had a picturesque way of honouring any woman who died unmarried; a white wreath, called the Virgin Garland, would be laid on her coffin during the service, and then hung in the church as her memorial. It is not clear how long ago this was done; Lower speaks of it as an eighteenth-century custom, abandoned when he writes (1861), but Augustus Hare, writing in 1896, says that many Virgin Garlands were still to be seen 'only a few years' before that date.

The custom of 'telling the bees' is well attested in Sussex. Bees, it was said, must always be treated as members of the family and kept informed of important news, particularly deaths and births. Someone ought to go out to the hives, tap each gently with the front-door key, and tell the news; some say one ought also to put black crape on them after a death, and white ribbon for a joyful event. If the bees were not told of a death, another death would soon follow in the household; while if they were not told of a birth, the child might die, or might grow up unable to digest honey. Other people said it was the bees themselves which might pine and die after such neglect, as they also might if one quarrelled about them or even spoke roughly in their presence, for 'they can't bear angry voices'. Others said they would never thrive if they knew they had been bought, and therefore it would be better to exchange them for a bushel of wheat. If money did change hands it must be paid over out of sight of the hives; such money ought also to be a gold coin.

Related ideas are by no means forgotten even now. A man living at East Dean came upon the belief in the 1950s when his father died, for a neighbour then asked him if his father's bees had been told of the death. He said no. 'Oh,' said the neighbour, 'I was going to offer to buy them, but I shan't now, as they won't be no good.' And in fact, all the bees did die.

It is just as important that bees should be told if they change hands. During the Second World War, a couple living at High Hurstwood decided to keep bees. Not knowing much about them, they asked advice from an experienced man in the village, who came and told them the best place in which to stand the hives; having placed them, he stood back and adddressed the bees : 'Now you've got a new master and mistress, and they are good folk, so see you work hard for them.' And turning to the owners, he added, 'They'll be all right now.'

Untoward behaviour by the bees might be put down to neglect

of this ritual. At Twineham in 1952, a woman who had just moved into a farm was plagued by the incessant swarming of her bees, bought from the previous farmer. She asked one of the men about it, and he asked whether the bees had been told that they had a new master and mistress. When she in surprise said no, he said 'I'll do it'. She watched him as he walked up and down in front of the hives talking to them, and when he had finished, the bees settled down.

Beekeeping is less common nowadays, and so no doubt these curious customs, the last survival of an ancient reverence for bees as intelligent and even holy creatures (pp 104–5 below), will soon be quite forgotten. But it is pleasant to think that when bees were still a common feature of country orchards and gardens they were treated as honorary members of the family, taking their place in the human life-cycle from the cradle to the grave.

10 The Turning Year

JANUARY

'WELL BEGUN IS HALF DONE', they say, so it is not surprising that there should be traditional rites to bring good luck to the beginnings of periods of time. One which was common in many parts of Sussex in the 1930s, and is still extant, concerns the first day of each month: if the first word you speak on waking up is 'Rabbits!', you will get a present before the month is out, while if you can add 'white ones with pink eyes' before anyone else has spoken to you, the present will be even better. Others say you should cry 'Rabbits!' three times, for good luck all through the month; and others too that, in addition, your last word the previous night should have been 'Hares!' Some families played a game of forfeits; if the children could say 'Hares and Rabbits!' to their parents before the latter said it to them, they claimed sixpence.

For similar reasons, the first glimpse of the new moon in January was once thought significant, either for good or ill; it must of course be greeted with the honours due to every new moon, such as bowing, curtseying, and turning one's money, and should never be first seen through glass, but in addition it could be used for divination. Writing in 1878, Mrs Latham records:

Should a girl wish to know what will be the personal appearance of her future husband, she must sit across a gate or stile and look steadfastly at the first new moon that rises after New Year's Day. She must go alone, and must not have confided her intention to anyone, and when the moon appears, it is thus apostrophised:

> All hail to thee, Moon, all hail to thee!
> I pray thee, good Moon, reveal to me
> This night who my husband must be. ·

I know of no recent instance of this charm being tried, but I do hear that the new January moon is still watched by our Sussex maidens.

Rather less poetic is the belief recorded by Parish in 1875 that in January it is lucky to bring mud into the house (presumably on one's shoes), and that mud is called 'January butter'. Judging by parallels concerning sand or dust elsewhere in England, the underlying idea would be that to bring something *into* the house, especially on New Year's Day, means bringing luck and wealth into the house all the year; sweeping or throwing things out, in contrast, would be unlucky.

A few special customs formerly marked New Year's Day itself. At Hastings in the 1870s apples, nuts, oranges and coins were thrown from windows for fishermen and boys to scramble for them. At the Red Lion Inn at Old Shoreham it was customary, throughout most of the nineteenth century, that a bushel measure should be filled with ale and decorated, and served free to all comers, at the brewers' expense. The *Sussex Daily News* of 5 January 1883 describes how it was done that year: the measure was decorated with green paper and flowers, and so full of ale that the head of froth loomed up among the greenery like a huge cauliflower; the ale was ladled out into pint glasses by a 'baler', and a chairman presided over the proceedings. The custom was clearly a form of wassailing, displaced from its more usual date of New Year's Eve or Christmas Eve (see below, pp 145, 149), since wassail bowls were often adorned with ribbons or greenery, and the ale ceremonially served out.

'Wassailing' has another meaning too; it is one of the names for the ritual of singing to apple trees, beating them, and pouring ale on their roots, formerly very popular as a way of ensuring a good crop in the following season. In Sussex, this ritual was also called 'howling', for reasons which will soon become clear. The most popular date for it was 5 January, Twelfth Night, but it could also be done on Christmas Eve, New Year's Eve, or Twelfth Day – indeed, any day between Christmas Eve and Old Twelfth Day (18 January) was a possibility.

The earliest reference to this ritual in Sussex is in 1670, when Giles More, Rector of Horsted Keynes, wrote in his diary on Boxing Day, 'Gave to the howling boys sixpence'. The custom was kept up in many villages during the nineteenth century, one of the best examples of its continued popularity being at Duncton. In 1906 a correspondent in the *West Sussex Gazette* wrote of Duncton :

> The chief wassailer there is Mr Richard Knight, who has discharged the duties for fifty-four years. Dressed in what some would describe as a grotesque costume, principally composed of patches rivalling the rainbow in multitudinous tints, the whole surmounted by an indescribable hat, bearing, displayed in front, a huge rosy-cheeked apple, he heads a procession of villagers carrying horns and such lowly musical types as bits of gas piping. Surrounding the largest apple tree, they chant :

> > Here stands a jolly good old apple tree.
> > Stand fast, root; bear well, top.
> > Every little bough,
> > Bear an apple now;
> > Every little twig,
> > Bear an apple big;
> > Hats full, caps full,
> > Three-quarter-sacks full!
> > Whoop, whoop, holloa!
> > Blow, blow the horns!

The custom was carried on until the 1920s by Richard Knight's son, 'Spratty' Knight, who in his turn acted as 'Captain of the Wassailers'. His daughter has recently described to Miss L. N. Candlin how the gang used to assemble at the inn and then go to each farm in turn, asking 'Do you want your trees wassailed?'

The gang, followed by numerous small children, then went to the orchard. Spratty blew through a cow's horn, which made a terrible sound. This was to frighten away any evil spirits that might be lurking around. Next, one of the trees, generally the finest one, would be hit with sticks and sprinkled with ale. This was a gift to the gods who looked after the fruit trees. Lastly all the company joined in the wassailing song, the words of which were as follows:

> Stand fast, root, bear well, top,
> Pray, good God, send us a howling crop.
> Every twig, apples big; every bough, apples now;
> Hats full, caps full, five bushel sacks full,
> And a little heap under the stairs.
> Holloa, boys, holloa, and blow the horn!

And holloa they all did, to the accompaniment of the horn. This completed the wassailing, and everyone trooped out of the orchard up to the farm-house door, where they were greeted by the farmer's wife with drinks and goodies. Sometimes money was given instead of good cheer . . . The next house visited was Lavington House, and then on around the village, visiting every house that had an orchard, till they arrived at the Cricketers' Inn, which was their last port of call.

Publication of this description in the *West Sussex Gazette* on 29 December 1966, stimulated further correspondence from people who remembered the Duncton wassailers, notably from Mr E. F. Turner, who grew up on one of the farms regularly visited, and who gave a vivid child's eye view of the proceedings. He remembered the wassailers approaching the farm in two different groups, chanting the lines of their song antiphonally, and sometimes specifying the species of the tree they were honouring ('Here stands a good Green Pippin tree', for instance). He remembered how 'they would come into the big kitchen . . . to sing songs and drink cider. One would be carrying the enormous cow-horn, and the Captain would have on a robe made of something like flowered cretonne, and a straw hat with big apples all round the wide brim, and a bow of wide ribbon.' The sing-song in the kitchen was a lengthy affair – 'people said they could remember enough songs to last for two hours or so' – and when at last the wassailers took themselves off to their next stopping-place, the farm children stood outside to hear their voices fading into the distance.

Such was the wassailing at Duncton; descriptions from elsewhere in the county add a few other traditional features, especially firing guns at the trees and beating them, and occasionally putting a bit of toast in the branches; the verses vary slightly. Sometimes, in places where there was no regular wassailing gang, a farmer might carry out the ritual for himself; in 1941 a contributor to the *Sussex County Magazine* recalled how his father, born at West Chiltington in 1836, used to recite the rhyme alone – 'deliberate emphasis was laid on each word, and the right hand was uplifted and circled on the last line'. In the same way, in 1964 a woman from Horsted Keynes remembered how, when she was a child, her grandfather would give her a penny to go and 'howl' to the apple tree in his garden and beat it with a stick.

Writing in 1827, T. W. Horsefield noted that beehives too were wassailed in some parts of Sussex, but the rite must have died out soon after his time, for all knowledge of how it was carried out seems to have disappeared. However, in the middle of the last century, the Rev G. A. Clarkson, then Vicar of Amberley, collected from an old man in his parish the words of a song which, it is thought, was sung to the bees on Twelfth Night:

> Bees, oh bees of Paradise,
> Does the work of Jesus Christ,
> Does the work which no man can.
> God made bees, and bees made honey;
> God made man, and man made money.
> God made great men to plough and to sow,
> And God made little boys to tend the rooks and crows;
> God made women to brew and to bake,
> And God made little girls to eat up all the cake.
> Then blow the horn!

The holiness here ascribed to bees is rooted in medieval

symbolism; beeswax is used in church candles, particularly the great Paschal candle which symbolises the risen Christ, and which in Roman Catholic ritual is blessed in a prayer alluding to 'the work of the mother bee'; honey is not only sweet but preservative, and is a Scriptural image of God's grace and of Heaven ('a land flowing with milk and honey'). The Sussex bee-wassailing song may well date back, in part at least, to medieval times.

Unlike wassailing, the traditional ceremonies for Plough Monday (the first Monday after Twelfth Night) seem almost unknown in Sussex. The only account I have come upon gives a vague dating, 'afore everyone had a bicycle', and does not name the village in question:

> When Plough Monday come along – that was the first Monday after Twelfth Night – all the Tipteers [i.e. mummers, see pp 146–8] used to dress all in white an' hang garlands of paper flowers round their necks, and bits of ribbon pinned all over, an' they dragged a plough round an' asked for money at every house. Then they had a festical [a feast] after, with beef an' plum pudding, an' the prettiest girl in the village was always chosen to sit at the head of the table. She was always called Bessie.

The description in fact shows a rather diminished form of the true Plough Monday rites, in which the 'Bessie' or 'Molly' was not really a girl at all, but a man in grotesque female clothing who accompanied the mummers on their rounds.

One farm at Horsted Keynes had a custom of its own to mark the beginning of the ploughing season, apparently unparalleled elsewhere in the county; it was called 'Winning the Cock', and a writer in 1927, drawing on his childhood memories, described it as follows:

> This took place on the first Monday in the year, when spring ploughing began. The carter's boy had to bring his whip into the kitchen on that day between sunrise and sunset, and thrash the table well, counting from one to nine while doing so. If he could do this three times, and get in and out of the house without having water thrown over him, he had 'won the cock'. Well do I remember the bowl of water that was kept ready, but only once was a lad successful. He was then solemnly presented

with three shillings and sixpence, which he transferred to his pocket with a great air of satisfaction.

For the rest, January lore is concerned with the weather, and is, naturally, depressing, being summed up in the belief that St Hilary's Day (13 January) is the coldest day in the year, and moreover that

> As the days lengthen,
> So doth the cold strengthen.

FEBRUARY

February weather is dismal too, always either frost or floods:

> February fill the dick [i.e. ditch],
> Every day black or white.

Yet it also offers the first few hints of spring – on Candlemas Day, 2 February, the first snowdrop appears, and some say the birds start courting on that day, though most say they wait till Valentine's Day, the 14th.

Two important movable feasts normally fall in this month, Shrove Tuesday and Ash Wednesday. Nowadays the former is of course marked by the almost universal custom of pancake eating and by a pancake race at Bodiam, but until at least the end of the eighteenth century it was chiefly marked, in many Sussex towns, by the cruel sports of cock-fighting and cock-throwing. Cock-throwing was a matter of hurling weighted sticks called 'libbets' from a distance at a tethered cock, which did however have room enough to dodge; whoever could stun the bird and pick it up before it recovered would have it as his prize.

A variant game, called Cock-in-the-Pot, was played in the Brighton Lanes. There, a cock was put in a large earthenware pot and strung up on a rope across the narrow streets, about sixteen feet up in the air; for the price of twopence one was allowed four shies at it with stout pieces of stick, and whoever broke the pot won the bird. There was a legend told to 'explain' the game, to the effect that it originated in Hastings in the days when the Danes ruled England. The oppressed Saxons had planned to massacre their masters, but the plot was spoiled by the untimely crowing of a cock, which woke the Danes too early. Later, when the oppressors had at last been driven out of the country, the English instituted this sport as their revenge on all cocks.

Such, at least, was the traditional tale; the game was played in the Brighton Lanes every Shrove Tuesday till 1780. The related customs were apparently dying out in the rest of Sussex at about the same period; the *Lewes Journal* stated in 1778:

> It is with great pleasure that we can inform the public that the barbarous practice of throwing at cocks is now so universally exploded in these parts that Shrove Tuesday did not produce a single instance of those acts of riot and cruelty by which the day was long and shamefully characterised, in open defiance of all humanity and all civic authority.

However, this reporter must have rejoiced too soon, for twenty years later, on 11 February 1799, the *Sussex Weekly Advertiser* thought it news worth noting that there had been 'no barbarous cock-throwing or cock-fighting' that year, these sports being 'totally abolished throughout the county'. It is to be hoped that this time they really were, but one author describing Mayfield as late as 1903 spoke of men then still living who remembered with gusto the cock-throwing they had taken part in in their youth.

A related custom which some old people still remembered in one (unnamed) Sussex village in the 1940s, was 'Thrashing the Hen'. This was a game played on Shrove Tuesdays by the servants at the local 'big house', and was a form of Blind Man's Buff:

> '. . . only they was all blindfolded 'ceptin' the Hoodman, and he had a hen in a sack, and bells tied to his coat-tails. All the others had sticks an' run after he, tryin' to beat him, an' he'd jump behind one of the others so he got hit instead . . . They was supposed to beat [the hen] to death, but Granfer says she didn't never get killed that way, but when they got tired of the game she was killed and plucked, an' then they all had her for dinner, boiled with plenty of fat bacon. An' then they had pancakes.

Ash Wednesday is marked, in some schools, by a custom of wearing an ash-tree twig; its white tip should be carefully blacked with ink or mud, and the children should not show anything white on their persons, for instance a handkerchief. Those who have no twig may, at any time up to the hour of noon, be pinched by the others, or even have their feet trodden on by every child who does have one. The custom was quite widespread in the 1940s and '50s, and so may well be still extant.

But the most striking significance of Ash Wednesday in the secular calendar used to be that, in the days when street games were still possible, it marked the opening of the marbles season, both for children and for some adults, for instance the Brighton fishermen; the marbles season reached its climax and conclusion on Good Friday (see below, p 111), thus coinciding exactly with Lent. Other children's games that began on this date were bat-and-trap and tip-cat; both were played in streets and open spaces, to the considerable inconvenience of passers-by. This was also the skipping season, and this game too attained a wider significance on Good Friday.

MARCH

The first of March was notable for its peculiar association with fleas. Everyone apparently agreed that on this date the creatures woke up and began hopping about, and that this was therefore the moment to try to get rid of them, but the suggested methods differed sharply. In West Sussex, the dominant belief was expressed in the rhyme:

> If from fleas you would be free,
> Let all your doors and windows open be.

Consequently, people would get up before dawn to fling their doors and windows open with the cry 'Welcome, March!'; sometimes, also, the children would be given brushes and told to sweep all dirt away from the thresholds and windowsills. But some people, particularly in the eastern half of the county, recommended the opposite procedure, with the verse:

> If from fleas you would be free,
> On the first of March let your windows closed be.

The custom is still sometimes remembered, though presumably not acted on. For instance, an informant at Littlington in East Sussex said in 1965 that the reason the windows were always kept shut in March was that it was believed that the winds blew the fleas out of the thatch. The blustery winds of March are notorious, whence comes the saying that this month 'comes in like a lion, and goes out like a lamb'; indeed, as the prevailing direction of the wind is from the west, I have heard the sarcastic comment that if the people of West Sussex are opening their windows on this date, it is only natural that those of the East should close theirs. Moreover, the people of Arundel had at one time a method of their own – on this date they went and shook themselves on Arundel Bridge, in the belief that this would keep them free of fleas for the rest of the year.

Mothering Sunday, the fourth Sunday in Lent, would normally fall in March. However, it does not seem to have been much observed in Sussex in the old days, being more a custom of the West of England. In recent years, of course, it has become universally popular, and is much advertised by flower-sellers and the makers of greeting cards; the Church too has recently taken it up, with such pretty ceremonies as the blessing of small nose-gays for children to give to their mothers. Some writers declare that the name originally sprang from an old ecclesiastical rule that representatives from each parish should visit the Cathedral, their 'Mother Church', on this day. With this in mind, some clergy now make the parish church a focus of ceremonial on Mothering Sunday; thus, at Firle in 1948, the church was encircled by a long chain of children holding hands, in a ceremony called 'Clipping the Church'.

Palm Sunday, the sixth Sunday in Lent, is marked by the gathering of twigs of willows, sallows, and other catkin-bearing trees, particularly the kind known as 'pussy-willow'. These are regarded as the English equivalents of the palm-branches mentioned in the Gospel describing Christ's entry into Jerusalem, and are still much used as church decorations. At one time, young men used also to wear small sprigs of them in their buttonholes on this day. In the nineteenth century it was common for parties to go out into the woods to pick pussy-willow on Palm Sunday – a custom which, like so much popular merrymaking, tended to get out of hand. The *Brighton Herald* for 30 April 1831 reported that the people and farmers of Patcham had been greatly troubled on the previous Sunday, being Palm Sunday, by hundreds of people of both sexes who, on the excuse of 'going a-palming', had come out from Brighton and spent the whole day in breaking down and gathering all the willows or withies in the hedges that were covered with yellow flowers. In the evening they went to the local inn; here they drank excessively, so that the night ended with many brawls.

Palm Sunday was also one of the festivals for which a particular food was traditionally prepared – in this case, a rich buttery affair known as Pond Pudding. By rights, this ought to be cooked in a pudding cloth, not a basin, and made to the following recipe:

Roll out a thick piece of suet dough into a thick round-shaped piece, about the size of a dinner plate. In the centre place a large ball of butter, brown sugar, and spice; the quantities for a family-sized pudding are four ounces of butter, a big handful of currants, and a pinch of spice. Pull the suet crust up round the butter ball till the pudding looks like a big apple dumpling. Seal the top with a piece of suet crust. Tie in a floured cloth and boil for two to two and a half hours. When serving, cut a slice off the top, and there revealed is a lovely yellow pond of sugary butter. In some homes, the currants are put into the dough; the pond is then surrounded by a sort of spotted dick.

APRIL

This month opens, of course, with April Fools' Day, which is as dear to Sussex children as to those of any other county, but which is too well known to need description, and is in no danger of dying out. More unusual are various customs and beliefs formerly attached to the period of Holy Week and Easter.

Good Friday has always been an oddly inconsistent day in popular observance – to the church-goer, the saddest and most penitential day in the religious calendar, but to others, a day of holiday on which to indulge in certain traditional games. In Sussex, the chief of these were marbles, skipping, bat-and-trap and tip-cat, which were played on this day by adults in very many towns and villages, including Battle (which held a match against Netherfield), Brighton, Burgess Hill, Cuckfield, Ditchling, Seaford, Southwick and Streat.

January

February

March

April

May

June

Marbles was a man's game – indeed, it was more a ritual than a game, with a fixed season, beginning on Ash Wednesday and ending on Good Friday at noon, sharp. In the same way as most inns now have darts teams, during Lent they once had marbles teams. The grand climax to these games was a championship held on Good Friday morning, and in the nineteenth century the sport was so popular that Good Friday was often actually called 'Marble Day' – a name which is not yet forgotten among the older people. The last survival of the custom is the annual match still held at Tinsley Green, outside the Greyhound Inn, which is said to have been played there for over three hundred years; it is played to the old rules, including that of stopping on the stroke of noon.

Games of marbles were sometimes played in the village churchyard, as was the case at Cuckfield some ninety years ago, while in 1879 the Rev W. D. Parish noted that at Selmeston the men and boys were so eager for their game that they would play outside the church right up until service time, and then, as soon as the service was ended, would rush out again to resume their game; he remarked that people who would never dream of playing at any other time would play on Good Friday.

Another favourite Good Friday sport was skipping. In some villages men and women, adults and children, all enjoyed the sport equally; but in those where the men played marbles, the skipping would be confined to the women, who used their own clothes-lines for the purpose. It was group-skipping, not the individual kind; a long line would be swung by two people, while one or two more skipped in the middle; these were then joined by more and more, until a whole row was skipping in unison on the same rope, which never broke its rhythm. The skippers would keep at it till someone missed a jump, or till all were exhausted, in which case others would promptly take their places. The custom was immensely popular in Brighton among both children and adults, especially fishermen; ropes were frequently brought up from the beaches into the streets and the fish-market, and the day was known as 'Long Rope Day' or 'Long Line Day'. Some said the custom had been instituted in memory of the rope with which Judas hanged himself. It reached its peak of popularity around 1900, and then gradually dwindled, though it was not till the Second World War that the closing of the beaches finally killed it.

In the early nineteenth century, the Good Friday games at Hove were even more spectacular. Hundreds of people used to assemble at a large prehistoric burial mound which then stood on the outskirts of the town (it was levelled in 1856/7), and there they would skip and play various other games, including kiss-in-the-ring, singing:

> Hey diddle-derry,
> Let's dance on the Bury.

There were organised games of kiss-in-the-ring also at Hastings, Seaford and Southwick until around 1910, while at Brighton the favourite sports (apart from skipping) were bat-and-trap and tip-cat, neither of which, however, was strictly limited to Good Friday.

The only instance of egg-rolling that I know of in Sussex is recorded as having been a Good Friday custom. It used to take place at Old Shoreham, on a hill behind the church which was consequently called Good Friday Hill. Children and others would go there in procession, and then roll hard-boiled eggs, dyed in various colours, and also oranges, down the steep slopes.

The special food for this day was, and still is, the Hot Cross Bun. There was at one time a firm belief that these buns, and also any bread baked on this day, had various curative and protective powers. Small loaves baked on Good Friday were given to children for them to keep all the year, and it was said that they would never go mouldy – which is not very surprising, since good care was taken to bake them very hard. In many households a Hot Cross Bun would be kept all year for luck, hung up near the hearth, or stored in an airtight tin; it was said to protect the house from fire, and a few crumbs grated from it were sometimes given as medicine to the sick. Fishermen's wives would give their husbands a bun to take to sea to avert shipwreck.

Good Friday is also, at Hartfield, the appointed date for one of those picturesque charity doles which were often to be found in English villages. The custom is said to be carried out in obedience to instructions in the will of a certain Nicholas Smith. Legend alleges that he lived in the seventeenth century and was the son of a rich squire at East Grinstead; he is said to have roamed the country disguised as a beggar, and to have found no charity anywhere till he reached Hartfield. There, however, he was kindly treated, and so at his death he requested that he should be buried there, and left his great wealth in trust for the relief of the Hartfield poor. But the real origin of the custom remains obscure; some attribute it to an eccentric Hartfield man nicknamed 'Dog' Smith because he drove about in a cart drawn by dogs. The custom demands that immediately after the Good Friday service is over, the Rector and churchwardens walk to what is believed to be Nicholas Smith's tombstone in the churchyard, and lay out the money on it, the churchwardens calling out the names of each recipient.

Finally, one should mention that Good Friday is the traditional day for certain agricultural operations, notably the planting of potatoes and peas, and the sowing of parsley. Both practical and superstitious reasons are involved. On the one hand, potato-planting is such heavy and time-consuming work that it may well have been necessary (at a time when Saturdays off were unknown and Sundays strictly observed) for working men to devote one of their rare holidays to this task in their own gardens; on the other hand, it is sometimes said that Good Friday is the only day in the year when the Devil has no power, and hence the safest day to plant a vital crop. As for parsley, though it is easy to sow it is notoriously capricious and slow in germinating, so that some people say its roots go seven times to Hell and back before it will sprout; but if it is sown on this holy day, not only will it sprout quickly, but it will come up curly.

Easter Day itself has gathered fewer folk traditions. Many people followed, and still follow, the rule of wearing at least one new article of clothing (frequently a pretty hat) when going to church that morning. The customary food was roast lamb and mint sauce, in allusion to the Passover Lamb with its garnishing of bitter herbs. As for the charming belief that the sun, at its first rising on Easter Day, dances in the sky in honour of the resurrection, Sussex people in the nineteenth century had a variant of their own – they did indeed hold that the sun danced, but they added that nobody would ever see it, 'because the Devil is so cunning that he always puts a hill in the way to hide it'.

Turning from the religious calendar to the fixed dates of the secular year, the only one significant in Sussex is 14 April, the date of Heathfield Fair (locally pronounced 'Heffle Fair'); since 1827 at least, this day has been called 'Cuckoo Day', and the fair, 'Cuckoo Fair'. The story goes that all winter through, the cuckoos are all in the keeping of an old woman of rather uncertain temper; if she is in a good mood, she goes to Heathfield Fair with a cuckoo in her apron, or in a basket, and releases it there, so that from that date cuckoos can be heard calling all over Sussex.

It was believed that unless you turned the coins in your pocket when you heard the first cuckoo, you would be poor all year; while some added that if you were in bed at the time, either you or someone of your family would fall ill or die. Lumbago sufferers could get rid of their trouble by rolling on the ground at the first call, while others sought good luck by sitting down and removing their right sock or stocking. Since cuckoos arrive when the land is drying out after the winter rains, it was said that they cleared the mud away; a popular rhyme still known to country children, runs:

> The cuckoo is a merry bird, she sings as she flies,
> She brings us good tidings and tells us no lies;
> She picks up the dirt in the spring of the year,
> And sucks little birds' eggs to keep her voice clear.

Finally, a farmers' custom observed in some places. As was said above, potato-planting was one of the more massive tasks for the individual labourer, who needed time off from working for his employer in order to get his own plot planted. In Rottingdean at about the turn of this century some farmers used to give their men a half day off for this, and the occasion developed into something of a ritual:

The custom of having a Saturday afternoon holiday had not been introduced at that date [1900], but sometime during April the farmer would arrange for all general farmwork to stop at one p.m. on a Saturday, and the men would spend the afternoon in planting their own potatoes on a piece of farm land allotted for their use. Mr Brown, the farmer, allowed each man eight rods and each boy four rods of ground, in which he could plant enough potatoes to keep his family supplied through the winter . . . They were also allowed the use of the horses and ploughs to turn the ground and get them planted. This was known as Spud-Planting Saturday . . .

On Spud-Planting Saturday there would be a well-attended gathering of men and boys down in the tap room of the Black Horse to celebrate the evening on 'tater beer'. The slightest

opportunity for celebration was never missed, and Tater Beer
Night became a favourite annual event. Old Uncle Tommy, the
landlord, used to put an enamel bowl on the counter, so that
every man made a contribution to the cost of the evening's
refreshment. Each man threw in a penny for every rod of
ground he had planted that afternoon; so a man with two boys
living at home would throw in one and fourpence – that is,
eightpence for his own piece and fourpence for each of the
lads. In this way there was soon enough in the bowl to start the
beer jugs going round . . .

Uncle Tommy would enter right into the spirit of the
evening, and used to put a pint pot on the counter and fill it up
with new clay pipes of all shapes and sizes – negroes' heads,
acorns, wrinkled pattern, or just plain. 'Help yourselves and pick
where you like,' he would say, and then he would offer a pot
of beer to the man who could sing a complete song in the
shortest time . . . Tater Beer Night was always one of the most
convivial evenings of the year.

MAY

> The First of May is Garland Day,
> So please remember the garland;
> We don't come here but once a year
> So please remember the garland.

This was the song of many Sussex children in the nineteenth
century, as they went from door to door through their towns and
villages, proudly displaying hoops covered in wild flowers, which
they called garlands; these were not for sale, but the children
hoped to be given a penny or halfpenny as a tribute to the
prettiness of the display. In Lewes, around 1875-85, children used
to go to Castle Bank, where their garlands would be judged by a
panel of ladies, and the best would be rewarded with a shilling;
the children had a half holiday for the occasion. As late as the
1920s, children went from door to door in Lewes in the old way.

A vivid description of various May Day customs in Horsham
in the early nineteenth century was given in his old age by Henry
Burstow, who was born there in 1826:

May Day, or Garland Day, was a very jolly time for us youngsters, not only because it was a holiday, but also because we used to pick up what seemed to us quite a lot of money. Early in the morning we used to get up our best nosegays and garlands, some mounted on poles, and visit the private residents and tradespeople. We represented a recognised institution, and invariably got well received and patronised. People all seemed pleased to see us, and we were all pleased to see one another, especially if the weather was fine, as it now seems to me it always was.

At Manor House special arrangements were made for our reception, and quite a delightful old-time ceremony took place. Boys and girls gaily decked out for the occasion, a few at a time, used to approach the front door, where a temporary railed platform was erected, and there old Mrs Tredcroft, a nice-looking, good-hearted old lady, used to stand and deal out to each and every one of us kind words and a few pence, everyone curtseying upon approach and on leaving.

Old Mrs Smallwood, who lived in a quaint old cottage in the Bishopric, always used to go round on May Day with an immense garland drawn on a trolley by two or three boys. On top of her garland she used to mount her little model cow, indicative of her trade – milk selling. Gaily dressed up herself in bows and ribbons, she used to take her garland all round the town, call upon all the principal residents and tradespeople, to whom she was well known, and get well patronised . . .

On this day, too, we had Jacks-in-the-Green. The chimney-sweeps used to dress up in fancy costumes and in evergreens and flowers, and, accompanied by a fiddler or two, parade and dance all round the town and neighbourhood. There were two sets of Jacks-in-the-Green when I was a boy, the Potter and the Whiting parties, and considerable rivalry existed between them. Lady Shelley used to patronise them handsomely, giving them plenty to eat and drink, and a good round sum of money. One year she gave the Whiting party a set of new dresses, fitting them out in a very gay manner. The children with their flowers and garlands finished their part of the proceedings about noon, but the Merry Andrew parties kept the game going all day, getting merrier and merrier as time went on, till the evening, when, the fiddlers still scraping away and now producing sounds so queer that it was comforting to reflect that they had no smell to them, they would all retire to Old Whiting's beer-shop and finish up.

The absence of a Maypole and Queen of the May, which are now usually thought essential to the celebrations, is not in fact very surprising at the period which Burstow is describing. May Day customs had to a great extent fallen into disuse in the first part of the nineteenth century, or been transferred to other dates, and it was not until the folklore revival towards the end of the century that picturesque ceremonials of Elizabethan times became common once again in English villages. But during the period of its comparative eclipse, May Day was still faithfully celebrated by a few specialised groups, notably (as here) by milkmaids, chimney-sweepers, and children. One of the last manifestations of the old, spontaneous custom (as opposed to organised processions, fetes, and so forth) could be seen in the groups of children who still came round to houses in Brighton in the 1930s, with paper flowers and paper ribbons stitched to their clothes, rattling a moneybox and chanting a corrupt version of the old rhyme:

> The first of May is Garland Day,
> The second of May is Washing Day.

The date was also important to Brighton fishermen, for if the beginning of the mackerel season should chance to fall upon it, this was regarded as a very lucky omen, and the boats would put out to sea bedecked with flower garlands. But in any case, on whichever day the mackerel shoals were first sighted, the fishermen would hold a celebration on the beaches off Market Street and Bedford Street on the afternoon before they set out to catch them; this they called 'Bendin'-In' or 'Bread-and-Cheese-and-Beer Day'. It was last held in 1896. Big baskets of bread, all hot, were brought down to the beach, along with baskets of round red cheeses, barrels of beer for the men, and ginger-beer for the children – all this being offered free to the fishermen and their families by the masters of the various boats. Sometimes, too, there was a Punch and Judy show. Those who carried on the custom explained the name 'Bendin'-In' by pointing out that the fishing nets were meanwhile 'bent up against one another', i.e. laid out on the beaches neatly folded up in the manner of a concertina. However, the name may well be a corruption of 'benediction', and may point to a pre-Reformation rite of blessing the nets at the start of an important fishing season.

Luck-bringing rituals were used during the actual fishing too. At Rye the fishermen simply spat into the mouth of the first mackerel they caught, but the Brighton men had a more solemn and religious custom. Every time they shot a net, the whole crew would stand bareheaded while the skipper prayed: 'There they goes, then. God Almighty send us a blessing, it is to be hoped.' As the tenth net, which was buoyed up with barrel floats, went over the side, the skipper would recite:

> Watch, barrel, watch, mackerel for to catch!
> White may they be, like blossom on the tree,
> God send thousands, one, two, three;
> Some by the head, some by the tail,
> God send mackerel and never fail;
> Some by the nose, some by the fin,
> God send as many as we can lift in!

When the last net was overboard, the skipper would announce 'Seas all!' He would take great care not to say 'Last net!', for if he did he would be sure never to see his nets again.

Despite its gay and auspicious beginning, May as a whole was once regarded by the superstitious as an unlucky month. For instance, a cat born in May was said to be inclined to melancholy, and to have the nasty habit of catching snakes and other reptiles and bringing them in the house. Taboos applying to this season include the idea that if you wash clothes on Ascension Day (normally a May feast) you will be washing away the life of one or other of your family; that if blossoms of the broom plant are brought indoors in May, then 'death will come with it'; and that:

> If you sweep the house with a broom in May,
> You'll sweep the head of that house away.

However, the month closed with another cheerful festival, Oak-Apple Day, 29 May, also known among children as Pinching Day or (to the horror of polite mothers) Pinch-Bum Day. This date is not only that of Charles ii's birthday but also the anniversary of his triumphant entry into Whitehall in 1660, on the occasion of his Restoration. To the popular mind, however, it is mainly the commemoration of his adventurous escape after the battle of Boscobel in September 1651, when he spent a night hiding in an oak tree. Sussex people have always felt a particular interest in this king's escape, since it was from Shoreham that he took ship for France; not surprisingly, the observance of Oak-Apple Day was enthusiastically kept up in most village schools at least until the 1920s, if not later. Children were expected to 'sport their oak', i.e. to wear oak leaves or an oak-apple pinned to their clothes. Those who did not would be pinched (preferably on the bum), or be struck across the back of the legs with a bunch of stinging nettles. The reason for the nettles seems to be lost, but the pinching was said to be in memory of a tradition that while King Charles was up his oak tree, his companion Captain Carless had to keep pinching him to stop him from falling asleep while Parliamentary troops were near.

In earlier centuries, 29 May was not merely an occasion for children's pranks, but an official public holiday. Until well into Queen Victoria's reign, the fishermen of Brighton used to decorate their boats with large branches of oak on this date, and a Brighton tavern called The King's Head was similarly decorated.

The civic festival of Mayor's Day at Rye comes towards the end of May, and on this day the Mayor and Councillors scatter hot pennies to children gathered in the street, who scramble for them. Two stories purport to explain this custom; one says it dates from the time when a Mayor of Rye was also a Member of Parliament, and bribed voters by scattering money; the other, that once, in the days when Rye had its own mint, the town ran out of pennies on Mayor's Day, and a boy sent to fetch new ones from the mint brought them back so fast they were still hot.

The major movable feast that normally falls in May is of course Whitsun. The traditional fare for this day was roast veal followed by gooseberry pudding, but the latter might present a bit of a problem if the feast fell early, before the berries were ripe enough; it was always a great disappointment if the Whitsun gooseberry pudding could not be made. The tradition is still kept up in some families.

Finally, it should be noted that Whit Monday has long been a popular and convenient date for such events as pageants, fetes, sports meetings, and the annual processions of benefit clubs and similar institutions. Such occasions sometimes include ceremonial features that are adapted from more ancient spring festival

customs. One such is the Whit Monday procession of the Harting
Old Club, which has been observed from 1812 to the present day.
A description written in 1953 tells how those taking part carry
peeled wands, ornamental staves, and flags; before the church
service they march in procession, anti-clockwise, round a large
beech bough which has been set up in the village square; after
the service, they enjoy a festive meal at the inn, and then a cricket
match completes the day's enjoyment. To the folklorist, the beech
bough is the most arresting feature in the ceremony, for the
fetching in of fresh leafy branches to set up as decorations was
an old form of May Day celebration; its reappearance in this
context is a good example of the way in which customs can be
transferred from one festival to another.

JUNE

In this month, there used to occur one of those major events of
the farming year which, while they entailed a great deal of
strenuous work, also gave an excuse for drinking and merrymaking
– in this case, the annual sheep-shearing. Until well into the
present century, the Downland farms were celebrated for their
huge flocks of Southdown sheep, the shearing of which required
far more labour than an individual farm could provide; consequently, men who were nimble with their hands (often including
town-dwellers such as tailors and cobblers, not merely shepherds
and farm workers) used to form themselves into a shearing gang
and tour a district, visiting several farms in turn.

The leader of each gang or 'crew' was styled Captain, and wore
some distinguishing mark in his hat, such as a gold band or a
couple of gold stars, while his second in command, the Lieutenant,
wore as his lesser mark a silver band or a single star. A typical
gang would contain some dozen or score of actual shearers, an
older man to stack the fleeces, and a young 'tar-boy' whose job
it was to dress the wound of any sheep that got cut with tar or
powdered lime, and to fetch and carry for the men.

The season would start with a gathering at a pub, called 'White
Ram Night', in the course of which the Captain would explain
to his crew the itinerary he had agreed on with the farmers, the
contracts he had drawn up on their behalf, and the rules they
were to work by – including a list of agreed fines for various

faults, such as swearing, leaving tufts unsheared, or letting a sheep wriggle out of one's grasp. The shearing season would last three or four weeks, during which time anything up to 10,000 sheep might be dealt with; the work was very hard, though it was often enlivened with evenings of drinking, singing and horseplay among the shearers, who would take up their quarters in the farmer's barn.

When their circuit was complete, the men repaired once more to a pub for the final (and far livelier) 'Black Ram Night', at which the Captain would preside over the final shareout of wages, and also the paying of fines; the latter would form a fund to pay for the evening's drinking. Needless to say, there were songs too that night; Bob Copper, whose great-uncle was Captain of a crew in Rottingdean around the turn of this century, describes the scene:

> The songs came thick and fast, for the more they sang, the more they drank – every song a drink was the rule – and the more they drank the more they sang. Frequently at the end of a song the whole company would join in this little chorus:

> A jolly good song and jolly well sung,
> And jolly good company everyone;
> And if you can beat it you're welcome to try,
> But always remember the singer is dry.

> Give the old bounder some beer.
> He's had some, he's had some.
> Well, give the old bounder some more.

> O half a pint of Burton
> Won't hurt 'un, I'm certain.
> O half a pint of Burton
> Won't hurt 'un, I'm sure.
> S.U.P.!

The songs often included the charming 'Rosebuds in June', and also the ever-popular drinking-game and song 'Turn the Cup Over', without which no rural festivity in Sussex could be considered really complete (see below, p 130). But, above all, they had to include 'The Sheep-Shearing Song' itself, in which some long-forgotten shearer has summed up all the essence of the hard work, high spirits, and communal feeling of the gangs, culminating in the joys of Black Ram Night itself:

> When all our work is done, and all our sheep are shorn,
> Then home with our Captain to drink the ale that's
>   strong;
> 'Tis a barrel then of hum-cup, which we calls the
>   Black Ram;
> And we do sit and swagger, and swear that we are men,
> But yet afore 'tis night, I'll stand you half-a-crown
> That if you don't have special care, this Ram'll knock
>   you down!

Of calendar dates, the only significant one in June is the night of the 23rd–24th, Midsummer Eve. Like other turning points of the year, this was thought to be a propitious moment for making contact with the unseen world, or divining the future. It was, for instance, sometimes believed that fairies could be seen dancing in their rings on that night, or that at midnight the cattle would kneel down in the fields. Girls who wanted to learn who they were fated to marry could carry out either of two well-known rituals, that of hempseed and that of the chemise. As regards the first, Mrs Latham noted in 1878:

It is some time since I last heard of any young persons seeking to ascertain their matrimonial fate by sowing hempseed, but the old belief still maintains its popularity. The maiden must steal out alone to the churchyard and sow a handful of hempseed and pretend to harrow it with anything she can drag after her, saying:

> Hempseed, I sow thee,
> Hempseed, I sow thee,
> And he that is my true love
> Come after me and mow thee.

She is then to look over her left shoulder to see a man mowing as he follows her.

The second form of divination for the same purpose is also described by Mrs Latham: a girl would wash her chemise and hang it up to dry in front of the kitchen fire just before midnight, leaving the kitchen door wide open; she would then wait in complete silence for someone to walk in and turn it – 'in one case, I was informed, a very tall man in black came in, and turned the sark, and slowly walked away'. Another method mentioned by the same writer was to go to a stream and dip the left sleeve of one's chemise into it.

These practices of almost a hundred years ago are presumably quite forgotten now, but the following type of divination described by Miss Candlin may well be still current:

> When we were children, we made Midsummer Men. These were two pieces of orpine, known to us as 'Live-long-love-long'. These we pushed through two empty cotton reels and took them to bed with us. One reel was given the name of our particular boy friend and the other was ourself. In the morning we looked at the reels. If the plants had fallen towards each other, all was well. If they had fallen one in one direction and the other in the opposite, then our love would not be true.

Midsummer Eve was also a likely date for the appearance of ghosts. Mrs Latham wrote:

> There stood, and may still stand, upon the Downs close to Broadwater, an old oak tree that I used, in days gone by, to gaze at with an uncomfortable and suspicious look, from having heard that always on Midsummer Eve, just at midnight, a number of skeletons started up from its roots, and, joining hands, danced round it till cock-crow, then as suddenly sank down again. My informant knew several persons who had actually seen this dance of death, but one young man in particular was named to me, who, having been detained by business at Findon till very late, and forgetting that it was Midsummer Eve, had been frightened (no very difficult matter, we may suspect) out of his very senses by seeing the dead men caper to the rattling of their own bones.

JULY

The July calendar contains two saints' days to which folklore is attached – St Swithin's, the 15th, and St James', the 25th. The best known belief about the former, still very often mentioned, though only as a joke, is that if it rains on St Swithin's Day it will rain for forty days thereafter. Less common is a belief that rain on this day 'christens' the apples, and is a favourable omen for a good crop; some people, indeed, assert that apples are never fit to eat unless St Swithin has christened them.

St James' Day, the 25th, at one time marked the start of the season for trapping wheatears on the Downs, since it was about this date that migratory flocks of these birds would visit Sussex on their way to Africa. Catching them was an important source of extra income to Downland shepherds, who sold them as a delicacy for the table. They were snared in T-shaped trenches cut in the turf, with a hair-spring in them, for they were such timid birds that they would fly into any available hole at the least alarm. But the 'birding' season was not marked by any particular ceremony or festivity at its opening; the feasting came later, in the form of a dinner given by some poulterers to the shepherds who supplied them with these delicacies.

This date is also that of the oddest and most interesting of Sussex fairs, the Ebernoe Horn Fair. This small village holds a fair on St James' Day, and challenges one or other of its neighbours to a cricket match. While the game is in progress, a whole sheep is roasted in the open air, on the edge of the village green, and at the end of the match the man who has scored the highest number of runs for the winning side is presented with the head and horns of the sheep to keep as a trophy. The custom is locally alleged to be 500 years old, though such a claim cannot of course be proved; what is certain is that after having lapsed 'for a great number of years', it was deliberately revived in 1864, and that since then it has been kept up with only one interruption – that caused by meat rationing between 1940 and 1954. Even during that interruption, it was at least sometimes possible to hold the cricket match itself, with a pair of antlers from the deer in Petworth Park as a substitute prize.

There is a folk-song associated with the Ebernoe Horn Fair, of which one version was noted down by Vaughan Williams in 1904, and another and better one collected from an old man, Jimmie Booker of Warnham, who died in 1951. This latter version is now sung every year at the Fair:

As I was a-walking one fine summer morn,
So soft was the wind, and the waves on the corn,
I met a pretty damsel upon a grey mare,
And she was a-riding along to Horn Fair.

'Now take me up behind you, fair maid, for to ride.'
'Oh no, and then oh no, for my Mammy she would
        chide,
And then my dear old Daddy would beat me full sore,
And never let me ride on his grey mare no more.

If you would see Horn Fair you must walk on your way,
I will not let you ride on my grey mare today;
You'd rumple all my muslin and uncurl my hair,
And leave me all distressed to be seen at Horn Fair.'

'Oh fairest of damsels, how can you say No?
With you I intend to Horn Fair for to go;
We'll join the finest company when we do get there,
With horns on their heads, boys, the finest at the Fair.'

The last couplet is probably to be explained as an allusion to some now long-forgotten custom, dating from an earlier period in the Fair's history, requiring those present to be dressed up with horns – that ancient symbol of cuckoldry which was a source for so many jokes from Shakespeare's time until well into the nineteenth century. Bawdy humour of this sort is exemplified in Sussex by the eighteenth-century Cock Fair at Ticehurst, at which, according to the *Sussex Weekly Advertiser*'s report of an unfortunate street accident which spoilt the fun in 1788, the landlord of the Cock Inn was 'according to annual custom presented with a load of wood, on condition that he could get it drawn home by men having the appellation of cuckolds, of whom he had assembled a sufficient number and provided them with a waggon for the purpose'. Whether the self-confessed cuckolds of Ticehurst were expected to wear the symbols of their state the newspaper unfortunately does not say; but a grotesque procession of this sort is known to have taken place regularly in Kent up to 1768, at the famous Charlton Horn Fair, which was notorious for its rowdy and bawdy goings-on, and where horns were prominently featured. The Ebernoe song, with its barely veiled allusions to seduction and cuckoldry, would fit well into such a context of licentious merry-making. It is to be feared that, if all were known, today's respectable cricket match and sheep-roasting would turn out to have a somewhat less respectable ancestry.

Charmingly innocent, by contrast, is Little Edith's Treat, which is held at Piddinghoe on 19 July. This celebration consists of a church service, children's races, and a children's tea, and was instituted in memory of a baby named Edith Croft who died in 1868, when she was only three months old. Her grandmother set up a fund of £100 in order that her memory should be preserved in this way.

AUGUST

August is nowadays a month without folk-customs, at any rate in Sussex, and has been so for some while. Not that it was a time of unrelieved hard work, even for farm labourers, but that what fairs and festivities there were (including, since 1871, the August Bank Holiday) did not develop any fixed rituals or ceremonies.

There was, however, one minor children's custom which could still be seen in Brighton in the 1860s, namely the building of 'grottos' of oyster shells on the street pavements on 5 August, to mark the fact that oysters were in season. The choice of date (which could in fact vary slightly) can be explained by the alteration of the calendar by eleven days in 1752; 5 August in the new calendar corresponds to 25 July in the old, and this last is the feast of St James, whose symbol is the pilgrim's scallop shell. The grottos were built of pebbles and shells, piled up about a foot high, and lit from inside by a stump of a candle; children would beg passers-by for 'a penny for the grotto', in the same way as they do nowadays for a Guy.

SEPTEMBER

In September (or sometimes late in August, if the weather was exceptionally kind), the harvesting would be over, and the farm workers could enjoy that most friendly and jolly of festivities, a Harvest Home or Harvest Supper. It was commonly held in the largest barn available, as soon as the last load had been carried in from the fields, and was, as Arthur Beckett once put it, 'an event celebrated for heavy feeding, curious songs, and big drinking feats' – and no wonder, for it marked the triumphant climax of the agricultural year.

But before the actual feast came the ceremonial of carrying in the last load, which has been described by several Sussex writers; it is often referred to as the 'Hollerin' Pot', in allusion to the cheering or 'hollering' of the workers, and the pot of ale with which they were rewarded. A simple form of the ceremony, as performed at Nuthurst in 1812 and 1813, is described by an eyewitness, H. P. Clark:

> When the last load of corn was to be brought to the stack, the bells were put on the horses, and when the last sheaf had been pitched, out came the bottle and glass, and each drank towards the health of the 'Maister' and 'Dame'.

A hundred years later the men of Challoners Farm, Rottingdean, were bringing in the harvest in much the same way, with a triumphant procession through the village, and cheers for the farmer and his family, as described by Bob Copper:

> On the last day of harvest, when all the barns were full and the rest of the corn was safely stacked, they used to celebrate by having the 'Hollerin' Pot' or 'Last Load'. The very last waggon would carry only a token load of just two layers of sheaves on the floor, and it would be decorated with flags and bunting slung between the corner poles. Jim [the author's father] used to sit up 'forard', as grand-dad had done in the old days when he had been bailiff, and the waggon would be drawn by a team harnessed up in tandem fashion, with the best horse from each of the four gangs, with each carter leading his own horse, and a boy riding on each of the three trace horses. All the rest of the company, sometimes as many as forty or more, would clamber into the waggon, ready to make the last triumphant and ceremonial journey down to the village, with the remainder of the waggons, carts and horses following on behind.

When they reached the crossroads at the lower end of the High Street, they would turn down towards the sea, right on to the cliff edge, and pull up in front of the old White Horse. Jim would holler:

I

'We've ploughed, we've sowed,
We've ripped, we've mowed,
We've carr'd our last load,
And aren't overthrowed.
Hip, hip, hip —'

and then a great Sussex cheer from fifty thirsty throats would
rattle round the valley, proclaiming the completion of a job
well and truly done. The landlord would come out with
members of his staff, carrying enough beer to go all round and
lubricate the cheering. His health would be drunk, and various
toasts would follow, such as 'God speed the plough' and 'may
the ploughshare never rust', and almost invariably someone
would break into song with 'The Brisk and Bonny Lad', or
another favourite that made reference to the harvest.

When the villagers in the street heard the singing, they knew
at once what it signified, and would stand at their open doors
and await the procession, falling in behind as it passed and
swelling the cheering, which grew progressively louder the
further up the village street they went. Halts were called outside
each of the public houses, the Royal Oak, the Black Horse, and
the Plough, where the rhyme and the mighty cheering brought
out the landlords with the same show of hospitality with which
they had been met at their first call.

After perambulating the village round by the Pond and into
the High Street again, they would finish up in the yard at
Challoners, where the farmer lived. He would come out to greet
them with his wife and daughters, and everyone would give
them 'a good old holler'. Then, after the horses had been
stabled, the whole company would adjourn to Challoners Court
Lodge, where there was an eighteen-gallon barrel of beer
stogelled up for the men, and crates of lemonade and ginger-
beer for the boys. Jim would tap the barrel, clear the tap, and
taste the first pot out, and if it met with his approval, which
can be taken for granted, he would raise the pot aloft and cry,
'Cocks and hens upon the midden, and by cripes she's a good
'un!' Then the drinks went round and the harvest would be
rounded off with robust celebrations which would not end until
the very last tawny drop had dribbled from the tap of that
rotund eighteen-gallon cask or 'kilderkin'.

On most farms, the owner would offer a festive supper to his men, often in the gaily decorated barn, within a day or two of the end of the harvest. The meal sometimes included such traditional fare as pumpkin pie and the large apple turnovers called 'brown georges'. According to Miss Candlin, seedcake was often served, and had indeed been readily available throughout the harvest season. This was because caraway seeds were believed to give strength very necessary to every worker at this time; they were also thought to provide protection against stealing, so that perhaps the eating of seedcake baked by the farmer's wife was a way of binding the loyalty of the farm workers to their master.

Whatever was served at the supper, it invariably culminated in toasts to the farmer and his wife, whether spoken or sung. One popular one noted down by H. P. Clark as having been used at Nuthurst in 1812 and 1813, and frequently quoted by later writers too, ran:

> Here's a health unto our Maister,
>   The founder of this feast;
> I wish him well with all my heart,
>   His soul in Heaven may rest,
>
> And all his works may prosper
>   That e'er he takes in hand,
> For we are all his servants,
>   And all at his command.
>
> So drink, my boys, come drink,
>   And see you do not spill,
> For if you do you shall drink two,
>   It is our Maister's will.

The toast to the farmers's wife, according to Clark, ran:

> Now we've drunk our Maister's health,
>   We will drink our Dame's;
> We'll drink and be merry, boys,
>   In drinking of the same.
>
> For him we have drunk one glass,
>   For her we will drink two,
> We'll drink and be merry, boys,
>   Before we all do go.

Soon after these toasts, the farmer and his family would withdraw, and the men would settle down to the really merry part of the evening – drinking, singing favourite songs, and keeping up traditional customs. The most popular of these, not only at Harvest Suppers but at sheep-shearing suppers and indeed every type of rural festivity, was 'Turn the Cup Over'. This has been described time and again by Sussex writers from the early nineteenth century onwards, and has remained a favourite almost to our own days.

It was supervised by a chairman, who had before him a large pail of beer, and was armed with a tall tumbler made of horn. The competitors would present themselves in turn, holding an inverted bowl or, in more recent times when very stiff and hard felt hats were common, a hat held crown upwards by its brim. The chairman filled the horn cup and handed it to the competitor, who received it on the bowl or the crown of the hat, without touching it himself; he then lifted the cup to his lips by raising the hat, and began to drink. As he did so, the onlookers, who up to now had remained solemnly silent, began to sing:

> I've bin to Plymouth and I've bin to Dover,
> I have bin rambling, boys, all the world over,
>   Over and over and over and over,
> Drink up your liquor and turn your cup over,
>   Over and over and over and over.
> The liquor's drink'd up and the cup is turned over.

The competitor had to time his drinking in such a way as to finish the beer just on the end of the fourth line; on the fifth line he had to jerk the empty cup into the air, still holding the hat only, then briskly reverse the hat and catch the cup in it as it fell. If he failed, the singers changed the last line to 'The liquor's drink'd up, but the cup *ain't* turned over.' The competitor then had to try again; naturally, the more often he tried, the less likely he was to succeed, but he had to keep it up, to the amusement of the company, till the chairman had mercy and let him off with a forfeit, and called for the next man. The game was kept up till everyone had had a go; sometimes, apparently, the chairman was expected to have a drink himself every time someone else did, a spectacle which must have added considerably to the amusement.

July

August

September

 *October*

 *November*

 *December*

Later in September, the nutting season began; St Matthew's
Day, the 21st, was called 'the Devil's Nutting Day', and indeed
the whole subject of nutting was entangled with semi-humorous
beliefs about the Devil (see above, pp 30, 65–6), which probably
reflect the opportunities for flirting which an afternoon in the
woods offered to young people.

OCTOBER

The Devil had a small share in October beliefs too, being supposed
to spoil all blackberries by spitting on them on the tenth of this
month, as has been described already (see pp 64–5); the chief
features of the month, however, were St Crispin's Day and, to a
lesser extent, Hallowe'en.

Some Sussex villages in the nineteenth century were as vigorous
in their celebrations of St Crispin's Day, 25 October, as of Guy
Fawkes Day, though the custom has now died out. This was the
particular feast day of cobblers, not in Sussex only but in many
parts of England, for Crispin was the patron saint of the Shoemakers' Guild; hence, it was a custom at Cuckfield for master
shoemakers to give a dinner to their employees on this day. But
there were many others besides the cobblers who celebrated this
feast, chiefly by bonfire customs of the sort that are so appropriate
to late autumn festivals. Thus, a correspondent writes in *Notes and
Queries* in 1852:

In the parishes of Cuckfield and Hurstpierpoint in Sussex, it is
still the custom to observe St Crispin's Day, which is kept with
much rejoicing. The boys go round asking for money in the
name of St Crispin, bonfires are lighted, and the day passes off
in very much the same way as the Fifth of November.

Local tradition in these two villages sometimes asserts that the
feast is kept up because one of the Burrel family of Cuckfield
fought at Agincourt, 'upon St Crispin's Day', and this attractive
and picturesque explanation was also offered at Slaugham, with
reference to the local Covert family. At Slaugham in the 1890s,
not only were there bonfires, but boys set tar-barrels alight, let
off fireworks, and ran round the village green waving blazing
brooms which they had begged for the occasion – or even stolen,

for it seems that on this night, as on Guy Fawkes Night, any combustibles left lying about were regarded as fair game.

To neglect the festival of the cobblers' saint would be punished by a form of ill-luck to fit the crime – or so we may infer from a rhyme current in Brighton in 1822, which was said to have been originally 'composed and vociferated . . . at an early hour of the morning through the streets and lanes', one Crispin's Day some forty years before that date, by a bell-man who was also a shoemaker:

> If ever I St Crispin's Day forget,
> O, may my feet be never free from wet,
> But every dirty street and lane pass through
> Without one bit of sole to either shoe!

At Horsham, as we learn from Henry Burstow's *Reminiscences*, the ceremonies had developed an extra and unusual feature – one of those semi-jocular, semi-cruel rituals by which rural communities punished those who offended against their code:

St Crispin's Day, the 25th October, used also to be well celebrated at Horsham, but it was regarded as an affair of the shoemakers, whose patron Saint Crispin was, and every one of them on that day could be depended upon to get thoroughly drunk in his honour. The townspeople generally were interested in the day because it was made the occasion for holding up to ridicule or execration anyone who had misconducted himself or herself, or had become particularly notorious during the year. An effigy of each offending person – frequently there were two together – was on Crispin's Day hung on the signpost of one or other of the public houses, usually in the district where he or she resided, until the Fifth of November, when it was taken down and burnt. For several weeks before the day, people would be asking, 'Who is to be the Crispin?'

The first 'Crispin' I ever saw was hanging outside the Black Jug in North Street when I was quite a tiny little shaver [i.e. in the 1830s]; I never heard whom it represented or what the man had done to get himself disliked. Another year the effigies of a man and his wife named Fawn, who lived in the Bishopric, were hanged up on the signpost of the Green Dragon. Together they had cruelly ill-used a boy, son of the man and stepson of the woman; they had also whipped him with sting-nettles. There they hung, each with a bunch of sting-nettles in the hand, till November 5, when a hostile crowd collected, some of whom went down to Fawn's house, assaulted him, and smashed his hand-cart. For this they were summoned and fined £2 each, an amount quickly covered by public subscriptions.

Another year old Skiver Tulley, the bootmaker, offended his brother stitchers. I never knew what he had done, but they suspended his effigy to old Whiting's sign-post, up at the beggars' lodging-house, on St Crispin's Day. Skiver came to Horsham from London, and being a particularly active and knowing member of the bootmakers' party, he was paid special honour: every evening from Crispin Day till the Fifth of November, the gentlemen of the wax [i.e. the cobblers] went up to the beerhouse, took the effigy in, and sat it down in the taproom, and then in its company all got drunk together.

The month of October ends with Hallowe'en, which, like Midsummer Eve, is an appropriate time for divinations of various sorts, for it too was an eerie time at which the worlds of seen and unseen might be expected to mingle. However, until recent years, it did not occupy anything like the same place in Sussex lore as in that of the Northern counties; only a few simple divinatory games were played by young people, in order to learn their marriage fate. One was with nuts; two nuts were laid in a bright fire, one supposedly representing the girl, the other the boy, and the player repeated:

> If he loves me, pop and fly;
> If he hates me, lie and die.

One would then watch the nuts, to see whether they burst noisily or merely smouldered away, the latter being a very unfavourable result. The divination by apples was equally simple; every person present fastened an apple to a string, hung up and twisted round before a hot fire. He whose apple fell first would marry first, and so in order; he whose apple fell last would never marry.

In recent decades, Hallowe'en has become much better known in Southern England than of yore; fancy-dress dances and children's parties are now common, usually with stress on the association of the date with ghosts, witches and devils, and children may be seen roaming the streets with turnip lanterns and eerie masks.

NOVEMBER

This month formerly had more popular customs than any other, and though only one, Guy Fawkes, is still kept up, some of the others only died out within living memory – for instance, the children's practice of 'going souling' on All Saints Day, 1 November. This is a very old custom, the original purpose of which (long since forgotten) was to assist the souls of the dead in Purgatory, who were to be commemorated on the following day, All Souls' Day; on the First, alms would be distributed to the poor as they went from door to door, and they in return would pray for the dead. Such a practice was of course impossible after the Reformation, but bands of people (latterly, only children) still went from house to house asking for 'soul-cakes'. They would be given a particular type of spiced bun, and sometimes a glass of milk or ginger-beer. Their begging-song ran:

> Soul! Soul! For a soul-cake!
> Pray, good mistress, for a soul-cake!
> One for Peter, two for Paul,
> Three for Him who made us all!

In Chichester a different tradition was observed, and one of which the symbolism was more appropriate to the actual feast day of All Saints. The shops were full of small iced cakes, and it was explained that the whiteness of the icing represented the white robes of the saints in Heaven, in whose honour these cakes were to be eaten.

Better known than any of these, and far more popular, were the Guy Fawkes bonfires and firework displays. There can hardly be a town or village in the county that did not have its communal bonfire, its processions of young men with flaring torches and blazing tar-barrels, and the continuous deafening uproar of the loudest possible crackers, bangers and jumping squibs – for it was the violence rather than the beauty of the fireworks which was appreciated.

The bonfire might be built on the market-place, the green, a crossroads, or any other more-or-less open space, with materials that had been gathered for days in advance and carefully guarded from rival gangs who might try to steal them. In some places, boys begged bits of wood from the householders –

> A stick and a stake,
> For King George's sake!

Those who would not give willingly might very well find their brooms missing later, or a few palings pulled from their fences. Indeed, on the night itself, one would be wise to keep everything burnable under lock and key, for as the fire sank lower, boys and men would rush about looking for something, anything, to keep it going. A night of such semi-licensed hooliganism was a splendid opportunity for paying off old scores; many an unpopular man would find his gates or shop shutters missing by morning. At Rye in the 1860s and '70s, things went further still; it was quite common for people to catch those they had a grudge against and tar and feather them, to the great amusement of the crowds.

Relations between the authorities and the revellers were, understandably, sometimes rather strained. The history of the Lewes Bonfires, the most famous and best attended in Sussex, has been marked in the past by several attempts to suppress it, leading to violent clashes between the police and the organisers, who were known there, and elsewhere, as the 'Bonfire Boys'. How heated tempers could become on this issue can be seen from a notice containing blood-curdling threats which was pasted up on Horsham Town Hall in 1779, clearly in response to some attempt to ban bonfires in the Square:

> Man, if you will believe us in advising you for your own good, all you that have the least hand in trying to prevent the fire and fireworks in the town would best come off, for it is determined between us to have a fire of some sort, so if you will not agree to let us have it in peace and quietness, with wood and faggots, we must certainly make a fire of some of your houses, for we don't think it a bit more sin to set your houses afire, and burn you in your beds, than it is to drink when one is thirsty. We don't do this to make a talk and chavash [i.e. chatter] about Town only, but so sure as it is wrote on paper, so sure by God Almighty we are in earnest. For we

should desire no better diversion than to stand at a distance and see your houses all in flames. Gentlemen, we shall take no money nor anything else to go out of the Square, for this is the place we have fixed upon.

But such violence and destructiveness were, fortunately, exceptional. For the most part, the Bonfire Night celebrations were thoroughly good-humoured, though extremely noisy. In many towns they were organised by several gangs of 'Bonfire Boys', each of which would head a carnival parade of men in fancy costumes, waving torches, dragging tar-barrels, and carrying Guys. Some Guys were huge, ten or twelve feet tall. On their way to the site of the bonfire, these processions would sometimes halt so that one of their leaders could deliver mock speeches denouncing unpopular politicians or foreign enemies, these being often identified with the Guys. The political element was particularly strong at Lewes, and it was there, more than anywhere else, that the anti-Catholic significance of the day was kept alive. Lewes had been the scene of the deaths of seventeen Protestant martyrs, burned to death in the days of Mary Tudor; consequently there was a marked streak of religious bitterness in its Bonfire Night celebrations until quite recent times, with speeches denouncing Popery delivered by mock 'Bishops' in surplice and gown. The traditional Guy Fawkes verses, elsewhere often shortened, would certainly be chanted there in their fullest version :

> Remember, remember, the Fifth of November,
>   Gunpowder, treason and plot;
> I see no reason why gunpowder treason
>   Ever should be forgot.
> Guy Fawkes, Guy, 'twas his intent
> To blow up the King and the Parliament;
> Three score barrels he laid below
> To prove old England's overthrow.
> By God's Providence he was catched
> With a dark lantern and lighted match.
> Holla, boys, holla, boys, make the bells ring!
> Holla, boys, holla, boys, God save the King!
> A farthing loaf to feed old Pope,
> A pennorth o' cheese to choke him,
> A pint o' beer to wash it down,

And a faggot o' wood to burn him!
Burn him in a tub o' tar,
Burn him like a blazing star,
Burn his body from his head,
And then we'll say old Pope is dead!
Hip, hip, hooray!

Such were the highly organised revels in the larger towns. But the villages had, and still have, their more informal celebrations. Occasionally these included curious little customs, archaic and inexplicable, which may serve to remind us that November bonfires are a very ancient ritual, far older than Guy Fawkes. Thus at Slaugham in the 1890s, the fire was always built up round a tall, stout green post, specially chosen so that it would char but not burn; it was called 'the scrag'. When the fire had died down, the scrag would be uprooted and carried away on men's shoulders; it would be taken to each of the two local pubs, and at each would be 'sold' for drinks – but what became of it in the end, we are told, 'was wropped in mystery'.

All in all, 5 November is a great day in Sussex. It is not surprising that the Hastings and Brighton fishermen, noting that shoals of herrings make their appearance off our coast at about this season, should declare that they come close inshore to see the bonfires. Similarly, the sprats, which appear slightly later, are said to come to see the Lord Mayor's Show in London on the 9th.

The next November date significant in folklore was Martinmas, the 11th, which in this century has been totally overshadowed by Armistice Day. At one time, however, it was quite important, particularly as a date for paying customary rents. There were also beliefs connecting it with the weather; thus it was said that there was usually a warm spell at this time, and if by any chance there was frost instead, this indicated that the rest of the winter would be abnormally mild:

If there's ice at Martinmas will bear a duck,
There'll be nothing after but sludge and muck.

A variant of this rhyme refers to 'Hallowtide', but whether this means 1 November, or, with allowance for the calendar change, 11 November, is not clear:

> If ducks do slide at Hallowtide,
> At Christmas they will swim.

St Clement's Day, 23 November, was the particular festival of all blacksmiths; they claimed him as their patron because he is said to have been martyred by being tied to an anchor and drowned. The forges were all closed, and early in the morning the smiths would 'fire' their anvils, to the delight of children, and the considerable alarm of horses. To do this, they put a little gunpowder in the hollow of the anvil, and lit it with a slow fuse. The noise of the explosion was meant to frighten off all evil spirits. The smiths would then go to a church service to ask a blessing on themselves and their tools, and in the evening would gather in some local inn to celebrate 'Old Clem'; the main dish would be a roast leg of pork, stuffed with sage and onions, and known as 'way-goose', and there would of course be drink in plenty.

In some villages and towns the smiths used at one time to make an effigy of their patron saint, representing him as an old man in a brown robe, with beard, wig, and clay pipe, and this they would set up at the door of the inn while their feast was in progress. In Brighton the custom was kept up only till the 1840s, but at Burwash, Steyning and Bramber it was still practised much later in the century; in 1926 Arthur Beckett described a conversation he had with an old woman from Bramber, who told him:

> We uster have some proper fun wi' Old Clem, I can tell 'ee. The boys made a figure which was meant for Old Clem, with a wig an' beard an' pipe in his'n mouth, just as if 'twere a real man. Then they put un in a chair, an' after firing off their anvils, they carried un round to all the houses, an' axed for apples an' beer. Arter they done that, they took the figure of Old Clem to the public, an' put un up agin the door while they had supper. A proper bit o' fun it was, to be sure.

Alternatively, one of the smiths himself might dress up as Old Clem and have himself carried in procession, enthroned on a chair and armed with a wooden hammer and anvil, while his mates carried various tools, and the procession was headed by a drummer.

Their feast was enlivened by toasts to various famous smiths
of ancient times – to Tubal-Cain, mentioned in *Genesis* iv, to
Vulcan, and of course to Old Clem himself. The toast to Vulcan
was ironical:

> Here's to Vulcan, as bold as a lion;
> A large shop and no iron,
> A big hearth and no coals,
> And a large pair of bellowses, all full of holes.

The proceedings invariably included a hearty rendering of the
'blacksmiths' anthem', variously known as 'Old Cole' or as
'Twanky Dillo', of which the first verse and chorus run:

> Here's health to the jolly blacksmith,
>> The best of all fellows,
>> Who works at his anvil
> While the boy blows the bellows,
> For it makes his bright hammer to rise and to fall,
> Says the Old Cole to the Young Cole to the Old Cole of all –
> Twanky dillo, twanky dillo, dillo, dillo,
>> Dillo, dillo, dillo,
> With a roaring pair of bagpipes made from the green
>> willow.

The blacksmiths, always very conscious of the prestige of their
ancient and highly skilled craft, had a legend which served at the
same time to explain the origin of the St Clement's Day feast and
to enhance their own status. The tale was told to Miss Candlin by
a blacksmith from Steyning:

> When King Alfred was on the throne, he called together all
> the tradesmen, and told them to elect one of their number to be
> king of the trades. There were then only seven trades, and a
> member of each was to attend at a certain time, complete with
> one of his tools and the product of his craft.
> The blacksmith came with a horseshoe and a hammer; the
> baker with a loaf and his peel; the shoemaker with a new pair
> of shoes and an awl; the carpenter brought a deal bunk and
> his saw; the butcher a joint of meat and a chopper; the mason
> his chisel and a cornerstone; and the tailor, having always been

an artful dodger, brought his scissors, and dressed himself in a new suit fit for a king.

When the rest of the traders saw the tailor, they at once voted him to be king, seeing that he was dressed for the part. All, that is, but the blacksmith. He knew without any manner of doubt who was fit for king, and in high dudgeon he exclaimed, 'You will see who is king when you break your tools! I won't mend them all the while that silly man is king!' And with that he went off and closed his forge, and all the other forges in the land.

Soon the men began to break their tools, and when King Alfred's own horse cast a shoe, it was really more than a joke. In desperation the men decided to break open the forge and to mend their own tools. But things went wrong right at the start. As the king began to shoe his horse and the tailor to mend his shears, the horse kicked the king and the tailor hit his thumb. The butcher lost his temper and pushed the baker. The baker pushed the shoemaker and the shoemaker pushed the carpenter. The carpenter pushed the tailor, and he, having no one else to push, fell against the anvil, which toppled over and exploded.

The noise brought the blacksmith to the door, and also St Clement, whose birthday it was. When the saint saw what a mess things were in, he tried to persuade the blacksmith to mend their tools. At last he relented, and did the work. The other tradesmen then said they had made a terrible mistake, and begged the blacksmith to be their king. The saint gave them his blessing, and because things had ended so amicably invited them all to a feast. At the feast everyone was in good form, except the tailor, whose nose was a bit out of joint, and while the rest were enjoying themselves he crawled under the table and snipped away at the bottom of the blacksmith's apron. That is why, to this day, a blacksmith has a fringe at the bottom of his leather apron.

As has already been noted, the blacksmiths of Steyning and Bramber took occasion of this feast to go from house to house 'to ask for apples and beer'. This custom, known as 'clemmening', was often kept up by children in places where the smith had discarded it; alternatively, they might go round two days later, on St Catherine's Day (25 November), in which case they called it 'catterning'. The children asked for 'apples and pears' rather than 'apples and beer', but the verse used was otherwise the same:

Cattern and Clemen be here, here, here,
Give us your apples and give us your beer [or pears];
One for Peter, two for Paul,
Three for Him who made us all.
Clemen was a good man,
Cattern was his mother.
Give us your best,
And not your worst,
And God give your soul good rest.

They would then be given fruit, nuts, cakes or sweets.

The last of the November saints is Andrew, with his feast on the 30th. Early in the nineteenth century, the bricklayers used to take their annual holiday on this day, and would go in gangs into the woods to hunt squirrels and other small animals by the primitive but effective method of stunning them with short, stout sticks; this they called 'going St Andring'. Afterwards, they went to an inn for a celebratory supper and drinking session. The dead squirrels were taken home to be eaten. This rather brutal custom grew rare in the course of the century, not out of consideration for squirrels, but because more land was enclosed as game preserves, and the gamekeepers did not relish the disorderly incursions of the bricklayers. But even so, the squirrel hunts lasted surprisingly long; one writer describing Mayfield in 1903 evidently knew of the custom, though on a different date, since when commenting on the disappearance of cock-throwing, he added, 'Would that the custom of squirrel hunting on Good Friday were also numbered among the things of the past!'

To turn to pleasanter subjects, the last Sunday before Advent has long been known, and still is, as 'Stir-up Sunday'. The collect for the day begins 'Stir up, O Lord, we beseech Thee, the hearts of Thy faithful people . . .' and this was jokingly associated with the idea that it was time for the housewives to prepare the mixtures for the Christmas puddings and pies, if they were to have time to grow rich and mellow by waiting. So, on the way home, the children sang:

K

Stir up, we beseech thee,
The pudding in the pot,
And when we get home,
We'll eat it all hot.

Next day, the grocers' windows would be filled with raisins, currants, spices, almonds, dried fruit, and all the other ingredients needed, and the women would set about their task. The actual stirring of these mixtures was a pleasant family ritual in which everyone took part. When they were already partially blended, everyone would be called in to help stir – mother first, then father, then the children in order of age, then all other members of the household, including servants, if any. Even babies stirred; the author has been informed that she stirred her first Christmas pudding in 1931, at the age of one. The way it was done was important; one must use a wooden spoon and turn it sunwise, from left to right – some say, because Christ's manger was of wood and because the Magi travelled sunwise as they searched for Bethlehem. And one should stir silently, with one's eyes shut, and make a secret wish.

The mince-pie mixture was also made in the week after Stir-up Sunday, and it too had some legends attached to it. For instance, many women put a little powdered rosemary into the mincemeat (which at one time included real meat, as well as fruit and spices) because of the tale that when Mary fled into Egypt with her Child, a rosemary bush by the wayside held out its branches for her to hang out the baby's clothes to dry on. At one time, too, the pies were baked in special little oblong tins with rounded corners, representing a cradle – no true Sussex cook would have made a round mince pie! The spicy filling represented the gifts of the Magi. And as for the eating of these pies, that is a subject to be considered under December.

DECEMBER

This month was, naturally, dominated by the approach of Christmas, but just before that great day there is another feast that was once of importance to the poorer sections of the community – St Thomas' Day, 21 December, popularly known as Gooding Day, or, sometimes, Doling Day or Mumping Day

('mumping' being an old slang word for 'begging'). As M. A.
Lower says, writing in 1861:

> Formerly, the old women of every parish went from house to
> house to beg something wherewith to provide for the festivities
> of Christmas. The miller gave each dame a little flour, the
> grocer a few raisins, the butcher an odd bit of beef, and
> so on. From persons not in trade a donation in money was
> expected.

Lower asserted that the custom was in his time 'almost obso-
lescent', but in this he was certainly mistaken; several other writers
mention it as prevalent in their own districts later in the nineteenth
century, and indeed it was not wholly extinct even in living
memory – the hardships of the elderly poor, especially widows,
are not so easily disposed of. Moreover, 'going a-gooding' was and
remained a serious custom, springing from real need, unlike the
more light-hearted 'clemmening', Guy Fawkes begging, or carol-
singing nowadays, though the latter, interestingly, is now often
done to raise money for charities.

The type of goods distributed varied. At Horsham, in the
nineteenth century, the gentry used to give out food, warm
clothing, and sometimes money; at Lewes in the 1870s, surplus
stocks of discarded clothes and hats would be left outside certain
shops, and anyone who needed them could take them; at Mayfield,
where the custom still existed in 1903, there was one old gentleman who had made it his life-long habit to save up all the
fourpenny pieces which came his way throughout the year, to
distribute them to the old women on Gooding Day. In one village,
the name of which is unfortunately not given in the source, the
widows went to church on this day with sprigs of holly or mistletoe,
which they handed to anyone who gave them money – a pleasant
fiction, no doubt, to soften stark 'charity' into a form of 'selling'.
Similarly at Beeding, in the first half of the nineteenth century, the
vicar used to sit at his study window handing out half-crowns to
any old woman who 'sold' him a sprig of evergreens. At Arundel,
on the other hand, the distribution of alms was official; the money
given out was the yearly interest on the sum of £15 which had
been found on the body of a dead tramp in 1824, and which had
been put into trust for this purpose.

As for the observance of Christmas, with its customary foods,

carol-singing, present-giving, Christmas tree, evergreen decorations, and so forth, it does not present any particular or unusual
features in Sussex. One picturesque custom, now presumably fallen
into disuse, was that of welcoming Christmas Day into the house.
In some families, the head of the house was expected to be the
first person to come down in the morning, and he had to set the
front door wide open and bid Christmas come in; in others, the
first person down had to take a broom, open the door, and sweep
trouble away from the threshold. There might well be some
competition for the privilege, as Mrs Latham implies, writing
in 1878:

> It is lucky to be the first to open the house door on this festival,
> and in my youth I was once persuaded by my nurse to get up
> with her before anyone of the family, that we might divide this
> luck between us, she throwing open the door that led to the
> offices [i.e. the back door], while I admitted Christmas by the
> front door, saying, as I had been instructed by her, 'Welcome,
> Old Father Christmas!'

Christmas was a lucky time in other ways too, as well as being
a holy season; for instance, those born on this day would never
be drowned or hanged. Part of the luck was connected with the
seasonal foods; in the nineteenth century some people liked to
keep a piece of the Christmas cake all year, and there is still a
widely known saying to the effect that every mince pie you eat
ensures a happy month in the following year – though some
people add that, for the charm to work properly, each pie must
have been baked by a different person. At a season where there
is much visiting to and fro, this condition is not too difficult to
fulfil for those at home among friends and neighbours, but in the
old days it did cause problems for young people working far from
home, for instance as servants or apprentices. So, to fulfil the
conditions, in large families one used to arrange that twelve
different people should each bake a batch of mince pies, and that
one pie from each batch would be put in a box and sent to any
member of the family who was away from home, to ensure him
his twelve happy months.

Christmas was also the season for wassailing, in several of the
senses of that rather elastic word. First, there was the wassailing
or 'howling' of apple trees, the season for which began on

Christmas Eve; this has already been described under 'January', since the most popular date for it was 5 January (see pp 102–4). Then, there was a form of 'wassailing' which was the direct ancestor of our modern carol-singing, though in earlier days the songs were not necessarily religious nor even particularly seasonal, to judge from a mid-nineteenth-century description:

> In Sussex there is a custom, celebrated at Christmas time, called wassailing. By this term is meant the singing of carols and songs by labourers going about from house to house. They are welcome at the fireside of the cottage, and are still admitted at the hall. The customary time for wassailing is from Christmas Eve to Twelfth Night. The men are dependent on oral tradition for their songs. Two of these commonly sung . . . are entitled 'The Baillie's Daughter of Islington' and 'The Blind Beggar's Daughter of Bethnal Green'; others . . . are 'A Sweet Country Life', and 'The Husbandman and the Serving-Man'. These ballads are not only remarkable as poetry, but are sung to very pretty tunes, probably as old as the ballads.

Another, rather unusual, type of wassailing was described to Miss Candlin a few years ago by a member of the Women's Institute at Shipley. She told how, when she was a child, the children would go round the village with gaily decorated baskets or china bowls covered with a cloth; in return for a penny or a cake, they would lift the cloth and let the giver have a peep at their 'wassail bowl'. Although there was nothing inside the bowl or basket, apart from decorations, this looks like a remnant of a more elaborate custom attested from several other parts of England in the nineteenth century, in which women or children carried round, hidden under a cloth, a lavishly decorated bowl or box with two dolls in it, these representing the Virgin and Child, and showed this to those who made a small donation. Perhaps the dolls were omitted at Shipley as being too Popish. Or, alternatively, the Shipley custom may derive from yet another form of wassailing, in which people took a decorated bowl of ale from house to house, offering a sip in return for a donation – though I find it harder to imagine how a good drinking custom should fall into decay, than how 'Popish' dolls might cause offence.

Boxing Day, 26 December, got its name, as is well known,

from the old and widespread custom of giving a money tip, known as a Christmas Box, to employees and tradesmen on this day – a custom now often replaced by the more practical habit of giving tips before Christmas rather than after. In Sussex traditions, the day is chiefly noteworthy as the favourite day for performing the Mummers' Play, though other dates within the Christmas period may also be chosen.

Mummers, in Sussex, are commonly called Tipteers or Tipteerers – a term the meaning of which is unknown. No fewer than forty-five of our towns and villages are known to have had, at one time or another, groups of men who performed the traditional Mummers' Play, going from house to house or performing outside inns. Many of the texts they have used have been recorded, in whole or in part; one of the more elaborate, from Compton, was printed by Arthur Beckett, and it is from this that my quotations will be taken.

The play, known in many other parts of England too, is in a mixture of doggerel verse and prose; it varies in length, but not in plot, and the speeches assigned to the various characters are also often very much alike in different versions. The subject is a combat between St George and a Turkish Knight whom he kills, and the latter's restoration to life by the skills of a comic quack Doctor. Subsidiary characters, found in some versions but not in all, include Father Christmas (acting as compère), other boastful champions named Valiant Soldier, Bold Prince, or Noble Captain, and the comic figures of Beezlebub or Little Johnny Jack, one or other of whom takes a collection from the audience. The plot is extremely simple, the tone comic.

In the Compton version, the action is introduced first by the Valiant Soldier:

> In come I, a roamer, a gallant roamer,
> > Give me room to rhyme;
> I've come to show you British sport
> > Upon this Christmas time.
> Stir up your fire and give us a light,
> And see we merry actors fight.

There is a second introduction from Father Christmas, in a speech beginning:

In come I, old Father Christmas,
    Perhaps welcome, perhaps not;
I hope old Father Christmas
    Will never be forgot.

After this, St George and the Turkish Knight both begin boasting of their strength and past exploits, threatening and defying one another, and fight. The Turk is killed at once, but the Doctor assures Father Christmas (who, it appears, is the Turkish Knight's father) that he knows a way to raise the dead. In rapid nonsense patter, he boasts of his skills, his travels, and his past marvellous cures:

I rose my poor old grandmother after she had been dead one hundred and ninety-nine years. She cut her throat with a ball of rice; I slipped in and sewed it up with a rice chain . . . I had a man brought to me the other day – indeed, he was not brought to me, he was wheeled to me, in a left-handed wheelbarrow. He couldn't see anything without opening his eyes, and he couldn't speak without moving his tongue.

The Doctor then revives the Turkish Knight with a few drops from a bottle of 'okum, slokum, elegant plaint' (or, rather more lucidly, in other versions, 'hocus, pocus, elicampane'). There follows, in the Compton version, a subsidiary fight between the Valiant Soldier and the Turkish Knight (neither gets killed), and the appearance of two clown-like figures, Beezlebub and Little Johnny Jack. The former carries a frying-pan, the latter a sack of dolls whom he calls his 'wife and family'. They too are braggarts, but their main function is to take up the collection. At Compton this was Beezlebub's task, as he appealed to the seasonal spirit of good will:

Christmas comes but once a year,
And likes to give you jolly good cheer . . .
Price, sir! Price, sir! And my old bell shall ring;
Put what you like in my old hat, and then these chaps
    will sing.

The performance then concluded with a carol.
    Descriptions of the Tipteers in the nineteenth and early

twentieth centuries show that they did not try to dress up in distinctive costumes suited to their parts, except that Father Christmas always wore a long false beard. On the other hand, they did not hide their identity behind the cascades of dangling ribbons worn by Mummers in some other parts of England. Some groups wore their ordinary working clothes, garnished with bits of coloured cloth cut out in stars or crescents or other designs, and had pheasants' tail-feathers in their hats; others had brightly coloured clothes, further decorated with spangles or knots of ribbon. The general intention was to be as gay as possible, but neither to disguise oneself nor to 'dress the part'.

In the present century, there have been several deliberate revivals of the play by groups of folk-dancers and other persons interested in old customs, but not necessarily in the same villages where the original bands of Tipteerers flourished. Notable among these modern groups were the Boxgrove Tipteerers, under the leadership of R. J. Sharp. Their version was a combination of texts from East Preston and Iping, written down in 1911 and 1912 from the memories of two elderly men who had been Mummers in their youth; it was performed at the Albert Hall in 1913 and again in 1937. After the Second World War the play was again revived, in a different version, by the Fittleworth Tipteerers. Indeed, performances still continue; the Chanctonbury Ring Morris Men gave the play on Boxing Day 1972 at Sompting and Steyning, telling the local Press 'We are empowered to bestow on our benefactors the gifts of good health, fine weather, fertility, and long sticks of red rhubarb'.

The Christmas season, and particularly Boxing Day, used also to be a time for a less agreeable custom – that of hunting the wren. Although at other times this bird was well enough liked for it to be considered most unlucky to disturb its nest, at Christmas in the mid-nineteenth century bands of boys used to go about beating the hedges and hurling 'libbets', i.e. short knobbed and weighted sticks, at any wrens which flew out. The origins of this custom (which has many more elaborate parallels in other parts of the British Isles) are mysterious and possibly very ancient; in its later form, however, it was only an outlet for brutal high spirits.

The last day of December is devoted to 'seeing the New Year in', by gathering to drink at home or in a pub, or by dancing in the street – at Chichester, in the days when traffic conditions allowed such things, the dancing was round the beautiful medieval

Market Cross. It was also (yet again) a day for wassailing apple trees, for instance at Horsted Keynes. But the most agreeable custom for this night is that of the Wassail Bowl, best described by Miss Candlin:

> In Sussex homes, as well as in the inns, the custom of wassailing was kept up until the end of the last century. Many wassail parties were held on New Year's Eve, and as the evening began to approach the hour of twelve, a large china bowl filled with hot spiced ale was brought in and placed in the centre of a round table in the middle of the room. On top of the ale floated 'lambs' wool' – the white fluffy inside of roasted apples, which looked like lambs' wool. Everyone present was given a silver spoon, and forming themselves into a procession, they walked round the table (clockwise), singing and stirring the ale at the same time. When the clock struck twelve, glasses were filled from the bowl, and everyone wished each other 'good wassail'.

11 Local Humour

PROBABLY MOST SUSSEX PEOPLE, at one time or another, have been teased by outsiders with the reminder that our county is saddled with the nickname 'Silly Sussex'. Many will have tried to explain it away by pointing out the etymology of the word – 'silly' comes from Anglo-Saxon *sælig*, 'blessed' or 'innocent', and the name therefore should be taken as a compliment. But this argument rarely convinces the mockers, and 'Silly Sussex' it remains, in the worst sense of the word.

But at least the county is no longer notorious for its mud, as was the case in the days of unmetalled lanes, deep in summer dust and winter mud. The latter was so glutinous that in 1751 Dr John Burton, in his *Essays of a Traveller*, asked himself:

> Why is it that the oxen, swine, women, and all animals are so long-legged in Sussex? May it be from the difficulty of pulling the legs out of so much mud, by the strength of the ankle, that the muscles get stretched and the legs lengthened?

To illustrate the incredible horrors of a Sussex lane, the following story was at one time a favourite : There was once a traveller
who, to keep as clear of the mud as he could, was wisely picking
his way along the top of a high bank that ran alongside a lane.
As he went his way, he noticed a rather good hat lying on the
muddy surface of the lane itself. It seemed a pity to leave it
there, so he cautiously stretched out his walking stick and hooked
it towards him – thus revealing, to his amazement, the head of a
man who was sunk almost to the eyebrows in the mud. The
traveller rushed off to get help, and a party with ropes arrived
and rescued the sunken man in the nick of time. The latter thanked
them heartily, and then asked whether they could by any chance
manage to haul out his horse, for when he was first seen he had
been sitting on horseback. 'Your horse?' they exclaimed in horror,
'Why, the poor beast must be dead, under all that mud!' 'Oh no,
he's alive right enough,' answered the other, 'for I could hear
him munching away at something down below. I think we must
have been stuck right on top of the big hay-wain which sank along
here last week.'

The small tight-knit rural communities of the past formed an
excellent environment for one particular form of folklore, the
traditional taunts and witticisms directed by people of one village
at those of another. This type of humour was once very widespread, and took the form of rhymes, nicknames, proverbial
sayings, and stock comments. The majority of them were noted
down in the late nineteenth and early twentieth centuries, and are
presumably much rarer nowadays; needless to say, they are quite
unjustified, and probably always were!

The joke sometimes turns on a verbal pun, as in the rhyme
about Rudgwick (pronounced 'Ridgick'), Wisborough Green,
Billingshurst and Horsham (formerly pronounced 'Horsam'), the
last-named being the chief victim :

> Rudgwick for riches, Green for poors,
> Billingshurst for pretty girls, Horsham for whores.

More often the humour is directed against some physical
peculiarity of the place in question. Amberley, for instance, is a
delightfully pretty village, but it is hemmed in by low-lying
meadows of the Arun valley, which until recent times were flooded
during much of the winter. Consequently, it was said that

Amberley people have webbed feet; that the women among them
have yellow bellies from lifting their skirts to warm themselves
over smoky fires; and that if you ask an Amberley man where he
lives he will answer cheerfully in summer, 'Amberley, where
would you?', but in winter gloomily, 'Amberley, God knows!'

> Amberley, God knows,
> All among the rooks and crows,
> Where the good potatoes grows.

   Such jeers were sometimes used as battle-cries by rival gangs
of village boys. One nineteenth-century observer happened upon
two gangs, one from Arundel and one from the tiny hamlet of
Offham a mile or so to the north, who were throwing stones at
one another and chanting insults:

> Ar'ndel mullet, stinking fish!
> You eats it off a dirty dish!

and:

> Offham dingers, church-bell ringers,
> Only 'taters for your Sunday dinners!

Another writer noted that people from Littlehampton taunted
those from Arundel with the same allusion to their local fish
(praised, incidentally, by Izaac Walton), 'Arundel mullet!' The
latter retorted, with reference to the ague-breeding marshes of the
Arun mouth, near which Littlehampton lies, 'Hampton shivers!'
   Other physical peculiarities commemorated in stock jokes are
the isolation of Thakeham, 'the last place God made'; the former
quietness of the cathedral town Chichester, 'where one half of the
people are asleep, and the other half goes about on tiptoe for fear
of waking 'em'; and possibly the hill-top site of Rotherfield,
where women are said to be so tall that they have an extra pair
of ribs.
   Other places have inexplicably acquired a reputation for moral
faults, such as pilfering and miserliness:

> The people of Fletching
> Live by snapping and ketching.

> Lewes men would skin a rat
> For to get its hide and fat.

There is a whole group of rhymes satirically alluding to village churches. Thus it is said of East Grinstead:

> Large parish, poor people;
> Large new church, no steeple.

Of Berwick, allegedly in reference to an actual event in 1811:

> The parson was poor and so were the people,
> So they sold the bells to repair the steeple.

Of Petworth, with reference to the old lead spire taken down in 1800, which used to lean askew:

> Proud Petworth, poor people;
> High church, crooked steeple.

Most scathing of all, of the free chapel at Playden, named after Sauket Street:

> Sauket church, crooked steeple;
> Drunken parson, wicked people.

Sometimes the butt of humour is not a town or village, but a particular group of people. Fishermen, for instance, are commonly accused of laziness because of the long hours they spend in enforced idleness, waiting for a good wind or tide. Hence it is said that Brighton fishermen have corns on their chests from leaning on the railings of the cliffs, and Hastings ones patches on their trousers from sitting down all day. It is also an insult to call the latter 'Chop-Backs', for this alludes to a bloody fight in 1768 between a gang of pirates based on Hastings and the crew of a Dutch ship, in which they savagely killed the Dutch captain by chopping his spine through with an axe. More obscure is the nickname 'pork-bolters' or 'pork-boilers' scornfully applied to Worthing fishermen, but it is perhaps connected with the fact that many seamen had a strong superstitious horror of pigs. Those of Eastbourne were also accused of an unsavoury diet, being taunted with the name 'willock-eaters' – the willock being the guillemot, whose flesh is most unpalatable.

The point of these sayings is indeed often conveyed by devious and mysterious hints. Thus, the comment on a braying donkey, 'Well, *he's* not from Rottingdean' constitutes a hit at that village's former reputation for smuggling – the idea being that Rottingdean donkeys were kept at work all night carrying contraband, so that they were far too tired in the daytime to bray. Equally oblique are the two possible Sussex rebukes to thoughtless people who leave doors open, namely 'Do you come from Yapton?' and 'Do you come from Seaford?' The latter is said to be an allusion to the extreme windiness of the bleak coast around Seaford, while the former has two traditional explanations, both derogatory – that the villagers of Yapton were so keen to avoid paying window tax that they bricked up all their windows and had to leave their doors open to get any light; or that they don't understand doors anyway, because they were all born in boats.

There is much controversy about the interpretation of certain old and puzzling jokes about the people of Piddinghoe (pronounced 'Piddenoo'). They are said to indulge in various apparently senseless occupations – they shoe magpies, they hang their fields out to dry, they fish for the moon, they go digging for moonshine, for daylight, or for smoke. On one level, these sayings can be taken simply as alleging that the people of Piddinghoe were utter idiots, for, as we shall see below, accusations of imbecility are a stock form of rural wit. However, a half-hidden meaning can be glimpsed in most of them. This village was a noted centre for the manufacture of chalk whitening, the chalk being ground up in water and then spread on sloping shelves to drain (hence 'hanging fields out to dry'); it was also once a smugglers' haunt, where kegs of spirits and tobacco ('moonshine', 'smoke') might well be buried or hidden in the river, to be dug up or fished up again later. As for 'shoeing the magpies', which has baffled most commentators, on one level it is merely a variant of a rural proverb 'to shoe the goose', meaning 'to attempt something futile or absurd'; recently, however, an elderly inhabitant of the village explained its inner meaning as alluding to the shoeing of the black and white oxen used for ploughing until early this century, these being locally known as 'magpies'. Finally, it is worth quoting a rhyme which must date from the Napoleonic wars, which hints at these villagers' prudent wish to avoid trouble and concentrate on their profitable trade of smuggling:

Englishmen fight, Frenchmen too;
We don't, we live at Piddenhoo.

Very different is the traditional image of Pevensey people – self-important, self-satisfied, boastful, and ignorant. Some anecdotes about them go back to the Tudor writer Andrew Boorde (who owned a house in the town), and others to Elizabethan times. The whole cycle probably first sprang from what must have seemed a ridiculous contrast between the town's theoretical status as a corporate member of the Cinque Ports, with its own Mayor and Court House, and its actual insignificance once the sea had receded from its harbour in late medieval times. Certainly the pomposity of the Mayor was a favourite target. One newly elected Mayor, says Boorde, graciously greeted a man who had doffed his cap to him with the words: 'Put on your hat, man, put on your hat! Though I am Mayor of Pemsey, I am still but a man!' Another, being illiterate, tried to read a letter upside down, and when the error was pointed out to him, he roared, 'Hold your tongue, sir! While I am Mayor of Pemsey, I'll hold a letter which way uppards I like.' It is also said that this Mayor, after laboriously deciphering a royal decree against persons maliciously firing beacons, went forth in all the majesty of his office to arrest a woman for frying bacon.

During the Napoleonic wars, Pevensey people are said to have boasted:

If Boneyparte should have the heart
To land on Pemsey Level,
Then my three sons with their three guns
Would blow him to the devil.

More recently jokes have been made hitting at their pride in their ancient Castle, of which one man is alleged to have said, 'I don't justly know how old it be, but it were here when I were a boy, an' I've bin 'ere a matter o' fifty year.' They are also said to be inordinately fond of the desolate expanses of Pevensey Marsh – 'A beautiful place, surelye! No hills, no trees, nor nothing to interrupt the view.'

Very many local jokes consist of pinning a reputation for idiotic stupidity onto inhabitants of a neighbouring district, and offering ludicrous anecdotes (which often fall into recurrent patterns) to illustrate the point. Among Sussex instances are the following: The men of Balcombe were jealous that the church of neighbouring Cuckfield had a higher spire than theirs, so they piled manure all round their own church to make its spire grow; at Storrington, people are so stupid that they have to go outside and look at a pond to see if it's raining or not; at Barcombe, when they want to make a cart, they make a waggon and cut it in two; at West Wittering, they sit up all night to wind the wind in with a winch, for fear there should not be enough wind to turn the sails of their mills next day. Such jokes are a traditional form of folk humour, which can be readily paralleled in other parts of England and indeed abroad.

Stories about alleged local fools tend to agglomerate into cycles, as has already been seen in the case of Pevensey and of Piddinghoe. Such a cycle has been elaborated in our own time by a Worthing humorist, Alfred Longley, centring upon an imaginary character named 'Jimmy Smuggles', whose adventures are partly devised as a satire on recent local events, but also in part based upon traditional jokes of the type described above. It has long been a standard witticism in Worthing to say of a man who has no obvious means of livelihood, and is suspected of being a lazy scrounger, that he 'works at Sompting Treacle Mine' – Sompting being a small village nearby. This remarkable mine, according to Mr Longley, was invented by 'Jimmy Smuggles', an imaginary personage whose knowledge and resourcefulness were a byword among workmen at about the time of the First World War.

Furthermore, Jimmy devised a way to lower the chimney of his mine so that the harvest moon could pass overhead without getting stuck on it, and also invented other weird industries such as a Porridge Quarry and the making of handkerchiefs for weeping willows. He and his friends tried to light their homes with bottled moonlight, and kept the sea salty with sacks of rock-salt; he once advised mill-wrights on Cissbury Hill to build only one mill there, not two, 'for there be only wind enough for one'; he taught some workmen how to lift a hole over a wall; and he foiled Napoleon's invasion by painting sheep red and massing them on the Downs. Jokes of this type have a long history in English folklore, and have sometimes achieved much more than merely local currency, as in the case of the famous Nottinghamshire tales about the Wise Men of Gotham; the numerous jokes about 'Jimmy Smuggles' collected and elaborated by Mr Longley prove, if proof were needed, that one traditional vein of English humour and fantasy is by no means exhausted.

Similar fantasy can be seen in the tall stories which countrymen loved to swap, partly for sheer fun, but partly in the hope that someday someone would be gullible enough to believe them. Several of these had to do with sheep and shepherding, and naturally were favourites with shepherds. There was one about a supremely clever sheep-stealer with a wooden leg, who wore a boot the wrong way round on his wooden leg, 'so the shepherd never knew if he was a-coming or a-going'. There was also the dramatic tale of the thief at Rottingdean who was actually hanged by a sheep which he had stolen. He had tethered it to a boulder on the cliff-top while he went for a drink, and later returned and fell asleep leaning against the same stone; during the night the sheep got its rope twisted round his neck and over the boulder too, so that by morning the thief was throttled. The boulder is still to be seen, and is known as the Hangman's Stone.

But the tallest of all is the tale of the Great Turnip. Sheep are very fond of turnips, and on Thorney Island the shepherds used to swop stories about the wonderful crops of turnips, or 'termits', on various farms where they had worked. On one farm, the shepherd was said to have lost a ewe during the winter – then, one day in early spring, he was folding the sheep over a field of very big 'termits'. He saw an extra large one, and went across to look at it. Peering through a large hole in its side, he saw his own lost ewe deep inside it, and a lovely pair of lambs with her!

But whatever jokes Sussex people may make at one another's expense, all would join in appreciating a story in which Londoners are made to look the fools, such as the tale 'The Mare's Egg', told to Arthur Beckett in the early years of this century:

Dunnamany year ago, two chaps what had come from Lunnon – a pleäce where all de men be as wise as owls – met a h'old Sussex man what was doddling along a roäd near his village wid a pumpkin under his arm. An' dese two Lunnon chaps didn't know what dis pumpkin was, as dey had never sin de loikes of un afore. So one on 'em says to de other, he says, 'Let's see what dis here ol' fellow's got under 'is arm.'

So dey goos up to un an' says, 'Good marnin', mister,' dey says.

'Good marnin',' says de ol' chap, friendly-like.

L

'What be dat under yer arm?' says de Lunnoners.

'Dat be a mare's egg,' says de ol' man.

'Dat so?' says de Lunnoners, believin' un loike lambs, 'We've never sin one so foine afore.'

'Yes,' says de ol' chap, 'dere be a mort o' common ones aroun', but dis 'ere one be a thoroughbred, an' dat's why 'tis so gurt an' foine.'

'Will you sell un?' says de Lunnoners.

'Wall,' says de ol' chap, hesitating-like, 'I doän't mind if I do, only I be dubbersome if you'll gi' me what I wants fur un; I ain't a mind to take less dan a golden sovrin' fur dis 'ere thoroughbred mare's egg.'

So arter dunnamuch talk dese 'ere Lunnon chaps dey gi' un what he axed, an' so he guv 'em de pumpkin, an' he says, 'Mind ye carry it careful,' he says, "cos 'twill hatch pretty soon, I rackon.'

'All right,' says de Lunnoners, 'we'll be careful.'

So off dey goos over de fields wud de mare's egg; and prensley him what was a-carryin' of it ketches his foot in a hole in de groun' so dat he dropped de pumpkin all of a sudden, an' dat starts a hare from de bushes, so dat it rip-an'-run down de hill. De chaps was dat vlothered dat dey was sure dat de mare's egg was hatched, so dey shouts out to some men what was workin' at de bottom of de hill, 'Hi! Stop our colt! Stop our colt!'

With which neat anecdote of a countryman's cleverness and townsmen's gullibility we may fittingly conclude this survey of Sussex traditional tales and customs.

Notes

Introduction, pages 11–16

Almost all the tales alluded to in the Introduction are given in full in the body of the book, and their sources will be found in the notes to relevant chapters. However, for the legends of King Alfred at Alfriston and of the Danes who crawled to Crawley see J. P. Emslie, *Folklore* XXVI, 1915, 163–5; for the battle of Terrible Down, see M. A. Lower, *S.A.C.* xv, 1863, 161, and J. Turle, *S.C.M.* IV, 1930, 893–4, 1067–8; for tales about Charles II, see M. Baldwin, *The Story of the Forest*, 1971, 17–18, and L. N. Candlin, *W.S.G.* 1 June 1967.

ABBREVIATIONS

S.A.C.	*Sussex Archaelogical Collections*
S.C.M.	*Sussex County Magazine*
S.N.Q.	*Sussex Notes and Queries*
W.S.G.	*West Sussex Gazette*

Churches, Bells and Treasures, pages 17–26

ALFRISTON: M. A. Lower, *S.A.C.* XIII, 1861, 226; also in many guide books. Lower notes that the same story was also told about Waldron, and Augustus Hare records a simpler version, without oxen, applied to Horeham (A. J. C. Hare, *Sussex*, 2nd edition, 1896, 95).
UDIMORE: T. W. Horsefield, *The History and Antiquities of the County of Sussex*, 1835, I, 510; also in many guide books.
HOLLINGTON: W. Diplock, *A Handbook for Hastings, St Leonards and their neighbourhood*, 1845, 7; C. Knight (pub.), *The Land We Live in*, c. 1847, I, 286.
BATTLE ABBEY: L. B. Behrens, *Battle Abbey under Thirty Nine Kings*, 1936, 32.
STEYNING: T. Medland, *S.A.C.* v, 1852, 113–14, summarising from *Acta Sanctorum Bollandi*, 1658.
MAYFIELD: M. A. Lower, *S.A.C.* XIII, 1861, 227.
BOSHAM BELL: A. J. C. Hare, *Sussex*, 2nd edition, 1896, 197; A. S. Cooke, *Off the Beaten Track in Sussex*, 1911, 168–70; A. Beckett, *The Wonderful Weald*, 1911, 228–9; see also articles by M. Rourke, F. B. Booth, J. Donne, and W. V. Cooke in *S.C.M.* XVII, 1943, 107, 175–6; XXIII, 1949, 254; XXIV, 1950, 252–4.
BULVERHYTHE BELL: F. E. Sawyer, *Sussex Place-Rhymes and Local Proverbs*, 1884, no. 24; L. N. Candlin, personal communication, 1971.
SELSEY BILL BELL: E. F. Harrison, *S.C.M.* IX, 1935, 265; his informant

was an old man from Selsey in about 1875, who claimed that his great-grandfather had once heard this bell. Miss L. N. Candlin informs me that the legend is still remembered (1971).

PETT LEVEL and KINGSTON GORSE BELLS : Informants at East Preston and Worthing, 1972.

BELLS LOST INLAND : At Isfield, M. A. Lower, *S.A.C.* XIII, 1861, 227–8, and G. Christian, *S.C.M.* XXVII, 1953, 190–2; at Etchingham, Lower, *ibid.*; at Hurstmonceux, A. S. Cooke, *Off the Beaten Track in Sussex,* 1911, 169; at Arlington, A. H. Allcroft, *Downland Pathways,* 1924, 62-3. For a theory that the name 'Bell Hole' is a corruption of *pell,* a dialect word for a deep pool, see D. MacLeod, *S.N.Q.* V :8, 1935, 229–32.

ALFOLDEAN (SLINFOLD) BELL : H. Burstow, *Reminiscences of Horsham,* 1911, 101; S. D. Secretan, *S.C.M.* XVII, 1943, 29–30, quoting oral accounts by John Pullen and an old man named Edwards, both of Rudgwick, who both died in the early 1930s; report in *W.S.G.* 15/7/65 of an interview with Stephen Peacock. See also reports and correspondence in *W.S.G.* 17/12/70, 1/7/71, 19/8/71, and 9/11/72 concerning the dowsing and excavation attempt.

THE GOLDEN CALF ON THE TRUNDLE : Brewer, *A Dictionary of Phrase and Fable,* 1870, 351, 761; W. D. Parish, *A Dictionary of Sussex Dialect,* 1875, 35, *s.v.* 'devil'; E. C. Curwen, *S.A.C.* LXX, 1929, 34; L. N. Candlin, *W.S.G.* 2/3/67; the Viking version, L. T. Crosbie, *S.C.M.* I, 1926/7, 534–5.

OTHER HILL TREASURES : At Clayton, L. V. Grinsell, *S.A.C.* LXXV, 1934, 238, and L. N. Candlin, *W.S.G.* 2/3/67; at Pulborough Mount, C. Latham, *Folk-Lore Record* I, 1878, 16, and M. M. Aldridge, *S.C.M.* XVIII, 1944, 306; at Chanctonbury and Mount Caburn (the knight), L. N. Candlin, *ibid*; at Mount Caburn (the coffin), E. C. Curwen, *S.A.C.* LXX, 1929, 34; at Firle Beacon, A. H. Allcroft, *Earthworks of England,* 679; at Wilmington, J. P. Emslie, *Folklore* XXVI, 1915, 163.

CISSBURY : C. Latham, *Folk-Lore Record* 1, 1878, 16–17.

TORBERY : H. C. Gordon, *The History of Harting,* 1877, 18; L. N. Candlin, *W.S.G.* 2/3/67.

CHIDDINGLY PLACE : M. A. Lower, *S.A.C.* XIV, 1862, 226.

Giants and Bogeymen, pages 27–33

THE LONG MAN OF WILMINGTON : The earliest reference to the figure is in 1779; for general surveys of the facts and theories, see J. B. Sidgwick, *S.C.M.* XIII, 1939, 408–20, and M. Marples, *White Horses and Other Hill-Figures,* 1949, 180–203; for the war-god theory, see C. Hawkes, *Antiquity* XXXIX, 1965, 27–30; for folk-legends about the figure, J. P. Emslie, *Folk-Lore* XXVI, 1915, 162–4; A. Beckett, *S.C.M.* x, 1936, 703; J. B. Sidgwick, *op. cit.,* 413.

LOST HILL FIGURES : T. C. Lethbridge, personal communication, 1963; J. P. Emslie, *op. cit.,* 165; A. H. Allcroft, *Downland Pathways,* 1924, 67; D. Harrison, *Along the South Downs,* 1958, 73.

GILL : A. L. Fox, *Archaeologia* XLVI, 1881, 426; J. Bellingham, *S.C.M.* XXVII, 1953, 423–7.

BEVIS OF HAMPTON : *The Gentleman's Magazine* I, 1833, 68; M. A Lower, *S.A.C.* IV, 1851, 31–6; F. H. Arnold, *S.A.C.* XXXIX, 1894, 214.

BOGEYMEN : Napoleon, E. L. Nourse, *S.C.M.* XII, 1938, 769, and L. N. Candlin, personal communication, 1971; the Danes, Helena Hall, in W. D. Parish, *A Dictionary . . . Enlarged, Augmented, and Illustrated,* 1957, 29; the Man in the Moon and the Devil, L. N. Candlin, *S.C.M.* XXI, 1946, 315–16, both threats having been commonly used by her grandmother.

SPRING-HEELED JACK : Helena Hall, *op. cit.,* 129; L. N. Candlin, *S.C.M.* XVII, 1943, with additional details given orally in 1971; her informant was her mother, and one of the boys her uncle. For a similar tale at Felpham, see G. Young, *The Cottage in the Fields,* 1945, 237–8.

CANNIBAL OGRES : M. A. Lower, *S.A.C.* XIII, 1861, 220–1; E. Shoosmith, *S.C.M.* III, 1929, 238–42; additional details concerning Sir Goddard, A. Hare, *Sussex,* 1896, and D. MacLean, *S.C.M.* V, 1931, 488–92, 451; J. Donne, *S.C.M.* XXI, 1947, 88–90.

Dragons of Land and Water, pages 34–42

ST LEONARD AND THE DRAGON : M. A. Lower, *S.A.C.* XIII, 1861, 223–5; Canon Tatham, *S.C.M.* V, 1931, 661–4; according to the latter, the lilies of the valley are more often said to spring from the dragon's blood than from the saint's, but other writers take the opposite view.

THE SERPENT IN ST LEONARD'S FOREST : The 1614 pamphlet is printed in full in E. V. Lucas, *Highways and Byways of Sussex,* 1904; see also M. A. Lower, *ibid.*; and S. Kaye-Smith, *The Weald of Kent and Sussex,* 1953, 113–14.

BELIEFS ABOUT SNAKES : M. A. Lower, *ibid.*; C. Latham, *Folk-Lore Record* I, 1878, 9, 12, 15–17; W. D. Parish, *A Dictionary of Sussex Dialect,* 1875, p 14, *s.v.* 'arder'; the cut snake or worm will not die till sunset, A. Sawyer, *S.C.M.* IX, 1935, 264, and childhood recollections of L. N. Candlin and myself; kill adder for victory, C. Latham, *ibid.,* 9, and G. Haskins, *S.C.M.* V, 1931, 122–3; the caduceus at East Grinstead, personal communication from L. N. Candlin, 1972.

BIGNOR HILL DRAGON : F. J. Bulstrode, *S.C.M.* III, 1929, 552.

KNUCKER-HOLES : *Notes and Queries,* 1855, 1st series xii 501; Helena Hall, in W. D. Parish, *A Dictionary . . . Expanded, Augmented, and Illustrated,* 1957, 71; bottomless pool at Lancing, E.O.H., *S.C.M.* XI, 1937, 475; Knucker Hole at Angmering, personal communication from L. N. Candlin, 1972, from an informant at Lyminster; ponds reaching Australia, Amy Sawyer, *S.C.M.* IX, 1935, 264; swallow-holes, W. Whitacker, *The Water Supply of Sussex,* 1911, 147.

WATER-HORSE AT RYE : L. Grant, *A Chronicle of Rye,* 1927, 154.

THE KNUCKER OF LYMINSTER : The version with a knight as hero is given by S. Evershed, *S.A.C.* XVIII, 1866, 180–3, by Canon Tatham, *S.C.M.* V, 1931, 661–4, and (in a very over-dressed version) by

A. Beckett, *The Wonderful Weald,* 1911, 395–402. The version with Jim Pulk as hero was kindly communicated to me (1971) by Miss Rosemary Anne Sisson, who heard it as a child in Lyminster in the 1930s, from a gardener, John Bishop. The version with Jim Puttock as hero is by C. G. Joiner, *S.C.M.* III, 1929, 845–6, from an account by an anonymous hedger from Toddington working at Lyminster. The setting of this version is in and around Arundel, a mile and a half north-west of Lyminster; Wick and Toddington are a mile or so south of Lyminster. Probably, despite the hedger's insistence that Puttock was from Wick, this version originated in Arundel – indeed the hedger himself remarked 'Some people says he was an Arundel man, but that ain't true.'

Graves and Ghosts, pages 43–51

BLACK DOGS, SPINNING WOMEN, SPINNING CALF : M. A. Lower, *S.A.C* XIII, 1861, 226.

GRAVES : The Miller's Tomb : oral traditions common in and around Worthing since the 1920s, or probably earlier, and still current. Toat Tower : information from a member of East Preston Young Wives' Group, 1972, whose mother came from Pulborough. Jack Fuller's grave, Brightling : F. John, *S.C.M.* II, 1928, 442–3; W. A. Bagley, *S.C.M.* XI, 1937, 172.

PREHISTORIC MOUNDS : A. H. Allcroft, *Downland Pathways,* 1924, 9–10; H. D. Gordon, *S.A.C.* XXVIII, 1878, 112; L. V. Grinsell, *S.A.C.* LXXV, 1934, 238.

KINGLEY VALE : A. S. Cooke, *Off the Beaten Track in Sussex,* 1911, 180–1; L. V. Grinsell, *S.A.C.* LXXV, 1934, 238–9; F. Venables, *S.C.M.* XI, 1937, 284; C. Woodford, *Sussex Ways and Byways,* 1968, 86.

HISTORICAL PERSONS : At Chanctonbury, J. Simpson, *Folklore* LXXX, 1969, 128–30; at Battle, B. Willard, *Sussex,* 1965, 187–8; at Bramber and Winchelsea, P. Underwood, *A Gazetteer of British Ghosts,* 1971, 38–9, 248; at Hooe, J. Hallam, *Haunted Inns of England,* 1972, 195; at Poling, D. Harrison, *Along the South Downs,* 1958, 234.

ST LEONARD'S FOREST : H. Dudley, *History and Antiquities of Horsham,* 1836, 45–6; M. A. Lower, *op. cit.,* 222–3.

WARBLETON PRIORY : A. Hare, *Sussex,* 1896, 96; J. Donne, *S.C.M.* XXI, 1947, 89.

TURKEY COCK LANE, RYE : A. T. Saville, *Ancient Rye,* 1891, 25–6.

JARVIS BROOK ROAD, CROWBOROUGH : B. Firmin, *An Illustrated Guide to Crowborough,* 1890, 141–2.

DAME SERGISON'S GHOST : M. Wright, *Cuckfield: An Old Sussex Town,* 1971, 110.

GHOSTLY DOGS : At Alfriston, see F. Pagden, *History of Alfriston,* 1895, 53; A. Beckett, *The Spirit of the Downs,* 1909, 215–19. Dog ghosts visible to other dogs, C. Latham, *Folk-Lore Record* I, 1878, 17. Black Dog Hill, Ditchling, personal communication from Miss Theo Brown, 1971, from an informant in Ditchling, 1960.

'WISH HOUNDS': B. Wills, *Shepherds of Sussex*, 1938, 100; on Ditchling Beacon, *S.C.M.* VII, 1933, 756; at Fairlight Cove, M. Thorpe, *S.C.M.* XXVII, 1953, 176–8.

THE DRUMMER OF HURSTMONCEUX: W. E. A. Axon, *Bygone Sussex*, 1897, 199–200; E. V. Lucas, *Highways and Byways of Sussex*, 1904, 337.

SMUGGLERS AT EDBURTON: N. P. Blaker, *Reminiscences*, 1906, 27.

THE PHANTOM HITCH-HIKER: From an oral informant in Worthing, 1971.

The Fairies, pages 52–60

THE SWEATING FAIRIES: M. Thorpe, *S.C.M.* XXVIII, 1954, 527–35; M. A. Lower, *Contributions to Literature*, 1854, 161–3; W. D. Parish, *A Dictionary of Sussex Dialect*, 1875, 41, *s.v.* 'farises'; C. Latham, *Folk-Lore Record* I, 1878, 28–9. A. Beckett, *The Spirit of the Downs*, 1909, 283, gives yet another version, in which a farmer says to the fairy, 'If you sweat for an ear, what would you do for a sheaf?'

THE BROKEN PEEL: M. A. Lower, *Contributions to Literature*, 1854, 158–61.

MASTER DOBBS: A. Beckett, *The Spirit of the Downs*, 1909, 283; L. N. Candlin, *S.C.M.* XVII, 1943, 96–7; H. Hall, in W. D. Parish, *A Dictionary . . . Expanded, Augmented and Illustrated*, 1957, 31, *s.v.* 'Dobbs'. The butter-churning charm is given by C. Latham, *Folk-Lore Record* I, 1878, 28, and by A. Beckett, *op. cit.*, 283.

FAIRIES LEAVE COINS: For maids, L. N. Candlin, *S.C.M.* XVII, 1943, 96–7; for children, J. Simpson, oral information from Worthing schoolgirls, 1965, 1972.

SITES ASSOCIATED WITH FAIRIES: Tarberry Hill, H. D. Gordon, *A History of Harting*, 1877, 19; Cissbury, Nancy Price, *Pagan's Progress*, 1954, 93; Pulborough Mount, C. Latham, *op. cit.*, 28; Harrow Hill, A. A. Evans, *S.C.M.* VIII, 1934, 432–4, on information from an old woman, who had had the tale from people 'before her time.'

RAISING FAIRIES: L. N. Candlin, *S.C.M.* XVII, 1943, 96–7; I. M. Stenning, *S.C.M.* XXVI, 1952, 430, from her nurse's childhood memories.

THE FAIRIES AND THE PIG: C. Latham, *op. cit.*, 27.

The Devil, pages 61–8

DEVIL SHUNS SUSSEX: B. Firmin, *An Illustrated Guide to Crowborough*, 1890, 131.

PLACE-NAMES: See Ordnance Survey maps; also, for the Devil's Bog, A. H. Gregory, *Mid-Sussex Through the Ages*, 1938, 14; for the Devil's Road, J. Middleton, *S.C.M.* XXIII, 1949, 282; for the Devil's Book, A. H. Allcroft, *Downland Pathways*, 1924, 24.

THE DEVIL'S JUMPS: L. N. Candlin, personal communication, 1971.
TORBERY (TARBERRY) HILL: H. D. Gordon, *The History of Harting,*
1877, 17; the story is still current (L. N. Candlin, personal communication, 1971).
THE DEVIL'S DYKE: This very well-known legend seems to have been
first mentioned in a late eighteenth-century poem by William Hamper,
and has been repeated in many guide-books from the 1830s onwards.
The subsidiary details about hill formations I have taken from H.
Belloc, *The Four Men,* 1912, ch. 2, and an oral version printed in
K. M. Briggs, *A Dictionary of British Folktales,* Part B, 1971, I,
89–90. For the ox-steddles, see A. H. Allcroft, *S.N.Q.* I, 1926, 65–70.
The details about the Isle of Wight and the Surrey Devil's Punchbowl
were respectively given to L. N. Candlin by a member of Poynings
Women's Institute in 1968 and to J. Simpson by an informant at East
Preston in 1972.
MAYFIELD: E. V. Lucas, *Highways and Byways in Sussex,* 1904, 334;
K. M. Briggs, *Pale Hecate's Team,* 1964, 230; for St Dunstan's Bridge,
see M. A. Lower, *S.A.C.* XIII, 1861, 221–2; for the Roaring Spring,
A. Hare, *Sussex,* 1896, 101; for Tongdean, B. Willard, *Sussex,* 1965,
93. The story about the horseshoes was told to L. N. Candlin in 1957
by a W.I. member at Mayfield.
BLACKBERRIES: C. Latham, *Folk-Lore Record* I, 1878, 14; L. N.
Candlin, *S.C.M.* XXI, 1947, 315–16.
NUTTING: M. A. Lower, *S.A.C.* XIII, 1861, 222; C. Latham, *op. cit.*;
L. N. Candlin, *op. cit.*; for the Tilehurst Woods story, T. Geering,
Our Parish, 1884, 145–8.
RAISING THE DEVIL: At the Devil's Humps, D. Harrison, *Along the
South Downs,* 1958, 262–3; at the Kingston tree, W. M. H. Luxton,
S.C.M. XXIII, 1949, 102, and L. N. Candlin, personal communication,
1971; at the Unitarian Chapel, I. M. Stenning, *S.C.M.* XXVII, 1953,
72–6; at Heathfield, G. L. Hall, *S.C.M.* XXIX, 1955, 27–8, on information dating from his mother's childhood; at Broadwater, told to
J. Simpson by Worthing informants, 1968 and 1971.
CHANCTONBURY RING: A. Beckett, *The Spirit of the Downs,* 1909,
131; for modern oral variants, see J. Simpson, *Folklore* LXXX, 1969,
122–31.
THE CROWBOROUGH WIZARD: B. Firmin, *An Illustrated Guide to
Crowborough,* 1890, 162.
MIKE MILLS' RACE: *S.C.M.* XV, 1941, 154–6.
CHARMS AGAINST THE DEVIL: L. N. Candlin, *S.C.M.* XV III, 1944,
261–2.

Witches, pages 69–78

THE HUNTED HARE: At East Harting, H. D. Gordon, *A History of
Harting,* 1877, 216; at Ditchling, Amy Sawyer, *S.C.M.* IX, 1935, 264;
at Duddleswell, B. Firmin, *Illustrated Guide to Crowborough,* 1890,
149; in various unnamed villages, S. E. Robinson, *S.C.M.* IX, 1935,

58–60; K. Harmer, *S.C.M.* xi, 1937, 451–2; M. M. Banks, *Folk-Lore*
LII, 1941, 74–5; I. M. Stenning, *S.C.M.* xxvi, 1952, 427–8.
OTHER TRANSFORMATION TALES : S. E. Robinson, 'Tom Reed : A
Man and his Lore', *S.C.M.* ix, 1935, 58–60; M. Fletcher-Jones, *S.C.M.*
v, 1931, 516. Tom Reed told his stories to S. E. Robinson in 1915,
or thereabouts. See also L. N. Candlin, *S.C.M.* xvii, 1943, 96–7; and,
for a tale with a natural explanation, L. E. Brown, *All About Bury,*
1948, 212; and G. Aitchison, *S.N.Q.* iv, 1936, 186–7.
THE WITCH AND THE WAGGON : M. A. Lower, *S.A.C.* xiii, 1861, 219;
at Ditchling, Amy Sawyer, *S.C.M.* ix, 1935, 264; at Plumpton, P. H.
Lulham, *S.C.M.* xiii, 1939, 36; at Stedham, J. Knight, *S.C.M.* xiii,
1939, 725; on the Surrey border, M. M. Banks, *Folk-Lore,* LII, 1941,
75; at the Sussex Pad, Lancing, S. H. Toms, *S.C.M.* ix, 1935, 332;
'Old Mother Venus', S. E. Robinson, *S.C.M.* ix, 1935, 58–60; the
witch and the Rector, A. R. Milton, *S.C.M.* xvii, 1943, 47–9.
HOLED STONES : A collection of these and other charms against witches,
made by S. H. Toms, is kept among the reserve collections of Brighton
Museum.
HORSES HAG-RIDDEN : K. Harmer, *S.C.M.* xi, 1937, 451–2; neither
the name of the informant nor that of the farm concerned is given. See
also C. Latham, *Folk-Lore Record* i, 1878, 24; A. H. Randell, *S.C.M.*
ix, 1935, 129–30; M. M. Banks, *Folk-Lore* LII, 1941, 75.
PIGTAIL BRIDGER : B. Firmin, *An Illustrated Guide to Crowborough,*
1890, 154–6.
THE WITCHES OF HARTING : H. D. Gordon, *A History of Harting,*
1877, 217.
COUNTER-SPELLS : At Crowborough, B. Firmin, *op. cit.,* 151-3; as
described by Tom Reed, S. E. Robinson, *S.C.M.* ix, 1935, 58–9; by
the bottle of pins, C. Latham, *Folk-Lore Record* i, 1878, 25–6; by a
hot poker, M. Beaumont, *S.C.M.* xxvii, 1953, 458, and B. Firmin,
op. cit., 150–1; by scratching, A. R. Milton, *S.C.M.* xvii, 1943, 47–9,
and C. Latham, *op. cit.,* 23–4.
AVOIDING WITCHES' SPELLS : S. E. Robinson, *S.C.M.* ix, 1935, 58–60;
A. R. Milton, *S.C.M.* xvii, 1943, 47–9; I. M. Stenning, *S.C.M.*
xxvii, 1953, 31.
DYING WITCHES : B. Firmin, *op. cit.,* 146–7, 153–4; S. E. Robinson,
S.C.M. ix, 1935, 59–60 (about 'Old Mother Venus'); about Nanny
Smart, A. H. Gregory, *Mid-Sussex Through the Ages,* 1938, 138
(from correspondence in a newspaper in 1895).
SOCIAL POSITION OF WITCHES : At Hailsham, T. Geering, *Our Parish,*
1884, 11–12; in an unnamed village, I. M. Stenning, *S.C.M.* xxvi,
1952, 247–8, with reference to the childhood of the writer's nurse.
At Hurstpierpoint, A. H. Gregory, *op. cit., loc. cit.*; at Hastings,
H. Cousins, *Hastings of Bygone Days and the Present,* 1911, 272;
the witch and the plums, M. M. Banks, *Folk-Lore* LII, 1941, 74; the
death of 'Betsey Shadlow' (a pseudonym, since the woman's daughter
was still alive in 1943), A. R. Milton, *S.C.M.* xvii, 1943, 47–9.

166   *Notes*

Healing Charms and Magic Cures, pages 79–88

The only detailed discussion of the subject is on pp 35–50 of C.
Latham's article in *Folk-Lore Record* I, 1878. Other sources used are
T. W. Horsefield, *History and Antiquities of Lewes*, 1824, II, 253–4
(silver ring for fits); W. D. Parish, *A Dictionary of Sussex Dialect*,
1875, p 15, *s.v.* 'axey' (ague cure by charm and by spider); J. Coker
Egerton, *Sussex Folk and Sussex Ways*, 1884, 107–9 (ague transferred
to aspen and goitre to snake, and potato for rheumatism); A. Beckett,
The Wonderful Weald, 1911, 273–4 (spider for ague); 'Wayfarer',
S.C.M. II, 1928, 186 (red flannel, red silk, potato for rheumatism,
horseradish for headache, frog for T.B.); G. Haskins, *S.C.M.* V, 1931,
122 (posthumous child to cure thrush, bread from 'John and Joan'
for whooping-cough, rooted bramble for boils, split ash for hernia);
E. Austen, *S.C.M.* IX, 1935, 596 (adder's oil); Anon, *S.C.M.* IX, 1935,
331–2 (woodlice for dropsy, whelps and worms for wounds, skulls
for epilepsy, bones for rheumatism, mice for diabetes and whooping-
cough); Anon, *S.C.M.* X, 1936, 122 (sheep for T.B.); W. Steele, *S.C.M.*
X, 1936, 514, (adder's oil); Anon, *S.C.M.* XIII, 1939, 237–9 (rabbit's
brains for teething, mice for whooping-cough, rooted bramble for fits);
P. H. Lulham, *S.C.M.* XIII, 1939, 55–8 ('wise woman' and diphtheria);
L. N. Candlin, *S.C.M.* XVI, 1942, 53 (hanged man's touch, snake
for goitre); I. M. Stenning, *S.C.M.* XXVI, 1952, 427 (ague tied to
tree); G. N. Slyfield, *S.C.M.* XXVI, 1952, 447 (thorn-tree at Portslade);
M. Beaumont, *S.C.M.* XXVII, 1953, 458 (mice for bed-wetting);
C. Woodford, *Portrait of Sussex*, 1972, 202–3 (mice for whooping-
cough, snail for warts, holed stone for scraping disease away).
The use of holed stones against nightmares and the account of
Janet Steer, the 'wise woman' of Lewes, were personally communicated
to me by Miss Candlin, whose mother (born 1870) was treated for
warts in her childhood by Janet Steer.

From the Cradle to the Grave, pages 89–99

INFANCY : C. Latham, *Folk-Lore Record* I, 1878, 11–12, 44, 46;
F. R. Williams, *S.N.Q.* X, 1944, 58; F. E. Sawyer, *S.A.C.* XXXIII, 257
(born on Sundays); E. Bell-Irving, *Mayfield*, 1903, 17 (born at
midnight); Anon, *S.C.M.* XVIII, 1944, 320 (biting baby's nails);
author's observation, 1960s (silver coin in baby's hand); C. Woodford,
Portrait of Sussex, 1972, 202 (rabbit's foot).
CHURCHING AND BAPTISM : C. Latham, *op. cit.*, 11–12; I. M. Stenning,
S.C.M. XXVI, 1952, 430.
HONEYSUCKLE STICK : F. R. Williams, *S.N.Q.* X, 1944, 58–62; L. N.
Candlin, *S.C.M.* XXIII, 1949, 154–6.
BANNS : J. Coker Egerton, *Sussex Folk and Sussex Ways*, 1884, 92;
L. N. Candlin, *S.C.M.* XX, 1946, 144–5.
WEDDINGS : T. W. Horsefield, *The History and Antiquities of Lewes*,

1824, II 249–50; M. A. Lower, *S.A.C.* XIII, 1861, 231; L. N. Candlin, *S.C.M.* XX, 1946, 144–5.

ROUGH MUSIC : M. A. Lower, *op. cit. loc. cit.,* (chaff-strewing); 'B.L.', *S.C.M.* II, 1929, 132 (at East Lavant); S. O. Woolley, *Folklore* LXIX, 1958, 39 (at Copthorne).

SMOCK WEDDINGS : *Sussex Weekly Advertiser,* 5 March 1770 and 10 November 1794, reprinted in *S.C.M.* IX, 1935, 102, and XXIV, 1950, 514.

SALE OF WIVES : *Sussex Weekly Advertiser,* 8 and 15 November, 1790; 17 July 1797; 25 February 1799; reprinted in *S.C.M.* XVI, 1942, 289, XXVII, 1953, 341, and XXIX, 1955, 94. H. Burstow, *Reminiscences of Horsham,* 1911, 73–4; *S.C.M.* I, 1926/7, 336.

DEATH OMENS : C. Latham, *op. cit.,* 51–61; P. H. Lulham, *S.C.M.* XIII, 1939, 55–8; *Folklore* XIV, 1883, 188 (heron at Chichester) ; L. N. Candlin, *S.C.M.* XXI, 1947, 130–1.

CERTAIN FEATHERS HINDER DEATH : C. Latham, *op. cit.,* 59; Anon, *S.C.M.* VIII, 1934, 701.

FUNERALS : Salt on coffin, I. M. Stenning, *S.C.M.* XXVI, 1952, 468. Wool in shepherds' coffins, B. Wills, *Shepherds of Sussex,* 1938, 195–6; A. C. Piper, *The Parish Church of St Andrew, Alfriston,* n.d., 8. Virgin Garlands, M. A. Lower, *S.A.C.* XIII, 1861, 231; A. Hare, *Sussex,* 1896, 124.

TELLING THE BEES : C. Latham, *op. cit.,* 60; M. Robinson, *S.C.M.* III, 1929, 698; G. Haskins, *S.C.M.* V, 1931, 122; M. Wyndham, *Mrs Paddick,* 1947, 132–3; L. N. Candlin, *S.C.M.* XXIII, 1949, 154–6, and personal communication 1972, from accounts given by informants in East Dean (1960), High Hurstwood (1956), and Twineham (1966).

The Turning Year, pages 100–49

JANUARY

'RABBITS !' : H. S. Toms, *S.C.M.* IX, 1935, 698–9; author's personal recollection from about the same time or a little later, and observation in Worthing, 1972; forfeit game, a Worthing informant, 1972, with reference to the 1930s.

NEW MOON : C. Latham, *Folk-Lore Record* I, 1878, 10–11, 30.

MUD : W. D. Parish, *A Dictionary of Sussex Dialect,* 1875, 63.

NEW YEAR'S DAY : At Hastings, T. F. Dyer, *British Popular Customs,* 1876, 11; at Shoreham, F. E. Sawyer, *S.A.C.* XXXIII, 1883, 238, and *Folk-Lore* I, 1883, 192–3.

WASSAILING APPLE TREES : W. D. Parish, *op. cit.,* p. 59, *s.v.* 'howlers'; P. H. Ditchfield, *Old English Customs Extant at the Present Time,* 1896, 46–7; at Duncton, G. W. Harfield, *W.S.G.* 11 Jan. 1906; L. N. Candlin, *W.S.G.* 29 Dec. 1966; E. F. Turner, *W.S.G.* 26 Jan. 1967; at West Chiltington, H. Greenfield, *S.C.M.* XV, 1946, 34; at Horsted Keynes, personal communication from L. N. Candlin, 1971. More general allusions to the custom in the nineteenth century can be found in T. W. Horsefield, *History and Antiquities of Lewes,* 1824, II, 267, and in the works of C. Latham and F. E. Sawyer cited above.

WASSAILING BEES : T. W. Horsefield, *op. cit. loc. cit.*; L. N. Candlin, *W.S.G.* 29 Dec. 1966. A shorter version of the rhyme was cited in *W.S.G.* 11 Jan. 1906.

PLOUGH MONDAY : M. Wyndham, *Mrs Paddick,* 1947, 130; at Horsted Keynes, E. Coomber, *S.C.M.* I, 1926/7, 117.

WEATHER LORE : L. N. Candlin, *S.C.M.* XXV, 1951, 18–19.

FEBRUARY

WEATHER LORE : W. D. Parish, *op. cit.,* 42, *s.v.* 'fill dick'; L. N. Candlin, *S.C.M.* XXI, 1947, 130–2.

COCK-THROWING : W. D. Parish, *op. cit.,* 69, *s.v.* 'libbet'; A. R. Wright, *British Calendar Customs* I, 1936, 22–3; at Brighton, L. N. Candlin, *S.C.M.* XXI, 1947, 284–6; at Mayfield, E. Bell-Irving, *Mayfield,* 1903, 16.

THRASHING THE HEN : M. Wyndham, *Mrs Paddick,* 1947, 137–8.

ASH WEDNESDAY : For twigs, see H. de Candole, *S.C.M.* XVI, 1942, 119; I. and P. Opie, *Lore and Language of Schoolchildren,* 1952, 240; the custom was also described to L. N. Candlin by an eighteen-year-old informant at Ringmer in 1950. For marbles and other games, see F. E. Sawyer, *S.A.C.* XXXIII, 1883, 240–1; R. Merrifield, *S.C.M.* XXVI, 1952, 58–63, 122–7; L. N. Candlin, *W.S.G.* March 23, 1967.

MARCH

FLEAS : C. Latham, *Folk-Lore Record* I, 1878, 49–50; Anon, *S.C.M.* XXVII, 1953, 106; L. N. Candlin, personal communication 1971, from information supplied by her grandmother, and by informants at Littlington in 1965 and at Arundel in 1954.

MOTHERING SUNDAY : Personal observations by J. Simpson and L. N. Candlin.

PALM SUNDAY : F. E. Sawyer, *S.A.C.* XXXIII, 1883, 240; *Brighton Herald,* 30 April 1831; Pond Pudding, L. N. Candlin, *W.S.G.,* 8 April 1965.

APRIL

GOOD FRIDAY GAMES : F. E. Sawyer, *S.A.C.* XXXIII, 1883, 241–2; M. F. Lindlay, *S.C.M.* IV, 1930, 429–30; L. N. Candlin, *S.C.M.* XIII, 1939, 272–3; R. Merrifield, *S.C.M.* XXVI, 1952, 58–63, 122–7; L. N. Candlin, *Country Fair,* April 1963, 41; L. N. Candlin, *W.S.G.* 23 March, 1967. Some villages did their skipping on Easter Monday, see Sawyer, *op. cit.,* and S. Bridger, *S.C.M.* XXVIII, 1954, 401. For marbles at Selmeston, see W. D. Parish, *Notes and Queries* V : 12, 1879, 18. For egg-rolling at Shoreham, H. Cheal, *The Story of Shoreham,* 1929, 256.

HOT CROSS BUNS : F. E. Sawyer, *op. cit.*, 204–1; E. M. Bell-Irving, *Mayfield*, 1903, 16; M. Hanna, *S.C.M.* XI, 1937, 187.
HARTFIELD DOLE : P. Tanner, *S.C.M.* XXIV, 1950, 138; F. Bunce *S.C.M.* XXX, 1956, 197 (with photograph).
EASTER SUNDAY SUN-DANCE : W. D. Parish, *A Dictionary of Sussex Dialect*, 1875, 57, *s.v.* 'Holy Sunday'.
CUCKOO FAIR : W. D. Parish, *op. cit.*, 32, 'Cuckoo-Fair'; C. Latham, *op. cit.*, 10, 17; F. E. Sawyer, *op. cit.*, 243–4; the earliest use of the name known to Sawyer was in Forster's *Pocket Encyclopedia of Natural Phenomena*, 1827. Cuckoo superstitions, Latham, *op. cit. loc. cit.*; P. Gosse, *Traveller's Rest*, 1937, 73; C. Woodford, *Portrait of Sussex*, 1972, 201; cuckoo rhyme, C. Latham, *op. cit. loc. cit.*, and L. N. Candlin, personal communication, 1971.
SPUD-PLANTING SATURDAY : Bob Copper, *A Song for Every Season*, 1971, 100–3.

MAY

GARLAND DAY : At Lewes, L. N. Candlin, personal communication, 1971, A. H. Allcroft, *Downland Pathways*, 1924, 55, and T. W. Horsefield, *History and Antiquities of Lewes*, 1824, II, 249–50. At Horsham, H. Burstow, *Reminiscences of Horsham*, 1911, 69–70. See also W. Holloway, *The History and Antiquities of Rye*, 1847, 608; and *The Brighton Herald*, 8 May 1824; for modern Brighton, L. N. Candlin, personal communication, 1971.
MACKEREL FISHING : F. E. Sawyer, *op. cit.*, 259–60; J. Hornell, *S.C.M.* XVI, 1942, 6–11; L. N. Candlin, *S.C.M.* XX, 1946, 84–6, from oral information from Dapper Twaites and others who remembered taking part in 'Bendin'-In'.
MAY SUPERSTITIONS : C. Latham, *op. cit.*, 17–18, 52; Anon., *S.C.M.* VIII, 1934, 567; A. R. Wright, *British Calendar Customs: England* II, 1938, 272 (a variant of the broom belief, in which the taboo is on using a brush made from broom twigs cut in May).
OAK-APPLE DAY : E. Shoosmith, *S.C.M.* X, 1936, 362; L. N. Candlin, *W.S.G.* 1 June, 1967.
RYE HOT PENNY SCRAMBLE : Anon, *Royal Pageantry*, pub. Purnell, 1967, 67.
WHITSUN FOOD : F. E. Sawyer, *op. cit.*, 246; L. N. Candlin, personal communication, 1971.
HARTING OLD CLUB PROCESSION : R. Merrifield, *S.C.M.* XXVII, 1953, 216–23.

JUNE

SHEEP SHEARING : R. W. Blencowe, *S.A.C.* II, 1849, 247–56; N. P. Blaker, *Reminiscences*, 1906, 5–8; M. Robinson, *A South Down Farm in the Sixties*, 1938, 10–12; L. E. Brown, *All About Bury*, 1948, 240–2; L. N. Candlin, *W.S.G.* 16 June 1966; Bob Copper, *A Song for Every Season*, 1971, 116–24. The Shearing Song can be found in

full in Blencowe, Blaker, Copper, or in B. Wills, *Shepherds of Sussex,* 1938; only Copper prints the tune.
MIDSUMMER EVE DIVINATIONS : F. E. Sawyer, *S.A.C.* XXXIII, 1883, 246; C. Latham, *Folk-Lore Record* I, 1878, 33–4; L. N. Candlin, personal communication, 1971.
FAIRIES ON MIDSUMMER EVE : F. E. Sawyer, *Sussex Natural History, Folklore and Superstitions,* 1883, 15; H. D. Gordon, *A History of Harting,* 1877, 19; N. Price, *Pagan's Progress,* 1954, 93.
CATTLE ON MIDSUMMER EVE : C. Latham, *op. cit.,* 17.
GHOSTS ON MIDSUMMER EVE : C. Latham, *op. cit.,* 20.

JULY

ST SWITHIN'S DAY : A. R. Wright, *British Calendar Customs: England* III, 1940, 34–5.
WHEATEARS : L. N. Candlin, *Country Fair,* July 1966, 35–6.
EBERNOE HORN FAIR : S. Goodman, *S.C.M.* XXIX, 1955, 320–3, 403, 501; the reinstitution of the fair in 1864 is reported in *W.S.G.,* 4 August 1864. A. Beckett (*S.C.M.* II, 1928, 331, 338) recalled that in his youth the horns used to be given as a prize for general open-air sports, not cricket. For Ticehurst Cock Fair, see *The Sussex Weekly Advertiser,* 19 May 1788, quoted in *S.C.M.* XIII, 1939, 739.
LITTLE EDITH'S TREAT : M. Gascoyne, *Discovering English Customs and Traditions,* 1969, 60.

AUGUST

GROTTOS : F. E. Sawyer, *S.A.C.* XXXIII, 1883, 248.

SEPTEMBER

'HOLLERIN' POT' : H. P. Clark, *Harvest Customs of Old Times, c.* 1830, reprinted in *S.C.M.* IV, 1930, 796; N. P. Blaker, *Reminiscences,* 1906, 8–11; Bob Copper, *A Song for Every Season,* 1971, 148–50; also E. M. Cannon, *S.C.M.* VII, 1933, 569, for the custom as carried out at Ferring and elsewhere in the 1840s.
HARVEST SUPPER : Food, L. N. Candlin, *S.C.M.* XX, 1964, 241–2, and *W.S.G.* 1 Sept. 1966. Toasts, H. P. Clarke, *op. cit. loc. cit.*; N. P. Blaker, *op. cit.,* 9; A. Dearling, *S.C.M.* XVII, 1943, 269, whose husband, born in 1853, had learnt the Master's Toast when young.
'TURN THE CUP OVER' : J. Rock, *S.A.C.* XIV, 1862, with tune; L. N. Candlin, *op. cit.*; Bob Copper, *op. cit.,* 122–4, in a shorter version omitting the last two lines.
DEVIL'S NUTTING DAY : A. R. Wright, *British Calendar Customs: England,* III, 1940, 77.

OCTOBER

ST CRISPIN'S DAY : *Notes and Queries* I: 1852, 30; F. E. Sawyer,

S.A.C. XXXIII, 1883, 250; L. N. Candlin, *S.C.M.* XIII, 1939, 672–3; J. Fergusson, *S.C.M.* XIII, 1939, 825; at Slaugham, M. Cooper, *S.C.M.* XXII, 1948, 354–8; at Horsham, H. Burstow, *Reminiscences of Horsham*, 1911, 76–7.

HALLOWE'EN: C. Latham, *Folk-Lore Record* I, 30–1.

NOVEMBER

SOULING: L. N. Candlin, *S.C.M.* XX, 1946, 265–6.

CHICHESTER ICED CAKES: Anon., *S.C.M.* VII, 1933, 646.

GUY FAWKES DAY: There are numerous descriptions of this in various towns and villages. For Lewes, see A. Beckett, *S.C.M.* II, 1928, 486–95, or *The Spirit of the Downs*, 1909, 204–25 (the former is his more detailed account). For Rye, F. W. Goodsell, *S.C.M.* III, 1929, 754; for Horsham, H. Burstow, *Reminiscences of Horsham*, 1911, 74–6; for Battle, J. Donne, *S.C.M.* XX, 1946, 282–3; for Rottingdean, Bob Copper, *A Song for Every Season*, 1971, 171; for Shoreham, H. Cheal, *The Story of Shoreham*, 1921, 254–5; for Slaugham, M. Cooper, *S.C.M.* XXII, 1948, 358. For the rhyme, A. Beckett, *S.C.M.* II, 1928, 495.

HERRINGS AND SPRATS: F. E. Sawyer, *S.A.C.* XXXIII, 1883, 251; L. N. Candlin, personal communication, 1971.

MARTINMAS WEATHER: F. E. Sawyer, *A Paper Read to the Sussex Natural History Society,* 1888; L. N. Candlin, *S.C.M.* XX, 1946, and personal communication, 1971.

ST CLEMENT'S DAY: W. D. Parish, *A Dictionary of Sussex Dialect,* 1875, 25–6, *s.v.* 'clemmening'; A. Beckett, *S.C.M.* I, 1926/7, 230–2; L. N. Candlin, *S.C.M.* XXI, 1947, 400–2, and *W.S.G.* . . .; F. Watts, *S.C.M.* IV, 1930, 339. 'Twanky Dillo' may be found in full in Beckett's article cited above, or, with tune, in Bob Copper, *A Song for Every Season*, 1971, 262–3.

ST CATHERINE'S DAY: W. D. Parish, *op. cit.,* 25, *s.v.* 'catterning'; L. N. Candlin, *S.C.M.* XX, 1946, 265–6.

ST ANDREW'S DAY: M. A. Lower, *S.A.C.* XIII, 1861, 215–16; L. N. Candlin, *S.C.M.* XX, 1946, 265–6; E. Bell-Irving, *Mayfield,* 1903, 16.

STIR-UP SUNDAY: L. N. Candlin, *S.C.M.* XX, 1946, 292–3, and *W.S.G.* 18 Nov. 1965; J. Simpson, personal recollections.

DECEMBER

GOODING DAY: M. A. Lower, *S.A.C.* XIII, 1861, 230–1; at Horsham, H. Burstow, *Reminiscences of Horsham*, 1911, 78; at Lewes, L. N. Candlin, personal communication, 1971; at Mayfield, E. Bell-Irving, *Mayfield,* 1903, 15; at an unnamed village, M. Wyndham, *Mrs Paddick,* 1947, 55–6; at Beeding, H. E. B. Arnold, *S.C.M.* XI, 1937, 406; at Arundel, F. E. Sawyer, *S.A.C.* XXXIII, 1883, 254.

LETTING CHRISTMAS IN: E. Coomber, *S.C.M.* I, 1926/7, 117; E. Canon, *S.C.M.* VII, 1933, 54; C. Latham, *Folk-Lore Record* I, 1878, 9.

CHRISTMAS LUCK BELIEFS: C. Latham, *op. cit.,* 9; F. E. Sawyer, *op. cit.,* 254; L. N. Candlin, *W.S.G.* 18 Nov. 1965.

WASSAILING TREES ON CHRISTMAS EVE: T. W. Horsefield, *The History and Antiquities of Lewes*, 1824, II, 267; at Chailey, W. Andrewes, *Old Church Life*, 1900, 67.
SINGING WASSAILERS: H. F. Broadwood, *Notes and Queries* 1:6, 1852, 600–1.
WASSAIL BOWL AT SHIPLEY: L. N. Candlin, *W.S.G.* 29 Dec. 1966.
TIPTEERERS (MUMMERS): The full list of Sussex Mumming Plays, with references, can be found in E. C. Cawte, A. Helm, and N. Peacock, *English Ritual Drama*, 1967; there are forty-five known instances, though the texts do not in every case survive. For the Compton text and performance, see A. Beckett, *S.C.M.* I, 1926/7, 547–52; for modern revivals, see H. Scott, *Secret Sussex*, 1949, 58–64; L. N. Candlin, *W.S.G.*, 6 Dec. 1967; *Worthing Herald*, 22 Dec. 1972.
HUNTING THE WREN: W. Borrer, *Birds of Sussex*, 1891, 80.
WASSAILING TREES ON NEW YEAR'S EVE: E. W. Swanton, *Bygone Haslemere*, 1914, 285; R. W. Blencowe, *S.A.C.* I, 1848, 110; C. Latham, *op. cit.*, 13.
WASSAIL BOWL ON NEW YEAR'S EVE: L. N. Candlin, *W.S.G.*, 29 Dec, 1966.

Local Humour, pages 150–8

THE HAT IN THE MUD: J. Coker Egerton, *Sussex Folk and Sussex Ways*, 1884, 58; A. Beckett, *The Wonderful Weald*, 1911, 159.
VILLAGE JOKES: F. E. Sawyer, *Sussex Place Rhymes and Local Proverbs*, 1884, has those about Amberley (webbed feet), Arundel, Balcombe, Barcombe, East Grinstead, Fletching, Horsham, Offham, Petworth, Piddinghoe, Playden, Rotherfield, Rottingdean, Seaford, and Thakeham. For 'Amberley, God knows!' see M. A. Lower, *The History of Sussex*, 1870, I, 8, and for Amberley yellow bellies, E. Porter, *Cambridgeshire Customs and Folklore*, 1969, 383, on the authority of an Amberley informant. For Berwick, see A. Beckett, *op. cit.* 230; for Chichester, Lewes, Littlehampton and Storrington, A. S. Cooke, *Off the Beaten Track in Sussex*, 1911, 284–5; for Yapton, C. Anscombe, *S.C.M.* XVI, 1942, 208–9, and A. Longley, unpublished material in Worthing Musuem; the latter also gives the joke about West Wittering.
JOKES ABOUT FISHERMEN: F. E. Sawyer, *op. cit.*; E. Partridge, *A Dictionary of Slang*, *s.v.* 'willock-eater'.
PIDDINGHOE: See F. E. Sawyer and A. S. Cooke, *op. cit.*, and also J. E. Lloyd, *S.C.M.* XXIV, 1950, 107–8. Interpretations are offered by Sawyer and Cooke, by B. Cleland, *S.C.M.* XXI, 1946, 265–6, and by L. N. Candlin, personal communication, 1971, from an informant in Piddinghoe in 1959.
PEVENSEY: M. A. Lower, *Chronicles of Pevensey*, 1846, 35–40; E. V. Lucas, *Highways and Byways of Sussex*, 1904, 332; A. Beckett, *op. cit.*, 62–3, 81; J. E. Lloyd, *op. cit.*
SOMPTING TREACLE MINE: The joke against scroungers was current

in Worthing in the 1930s and 1940s (author's personal recollection).
For the Jimmy Smuggles cycle, see unpublished poems, tales and
drawings by Alfred Longley, in Worthing Museum.

THE HANGMAN'S STONE : Bob Copper, *A Song for Every Season,* 1971,
58–60.

THE GREAT TURNIP : V. Lacey, 'Letter to the Editor', *W.S.G.* 6/3/1958;
also the wooden-legged sheep-stealer.

THE MARE'S EGG : A. Beckett, *The Wonderful Weald,* 1911, 274–5.

Select Bibliography

The following are the main sources for Sussex folklore, but not every book and article consulted is listed here; those in which only one or two items are to be found have been mentioned under the appropriate headings in the notes.

A. BECKETT, *The Spirit of the Downs*, 1909
   'The Sussex Mummers' Play', *S.C.M.* I, 1926/7, 545–52
   The Wonderful Weald, 1911
E. BELL-IRVING, *Mayfield*, 1903
H. BURSTOW, *Reminiscences of Horsham*, 1911
L. N. CANDLIN, 'Bat-and-Trap, Tip-Cat, and Other Games for Good Friday, *W.S.G.* 23 March 1967
   'Be You Superstitious Like?', *S.C.M.* XVIII, 1944, 261–2
   'Blackberry Pickers Beware', *S.C.M.* XXI, 1947, 315–16
   'The Brighton Lanes', *S.C.M.* XXI, 1947, 284–6
   'Buried Treasure in the Sussex Hills', *W.S.G.* 2 March 1967
   'Customs of Brighton Fisherfolk', *S.C.M.* XIII, 1939, 272–3
   'The Fight for Brighton Fishmarket', *S.C.M.* XX, 1946, 84–6
   'Marry in June', *S.C.M.* XX, 1946, 144–5
   'Old Wassailing Customs in Sussex', *W.S.G.* 29 Dec. 1966
   'Plant Lore of Sussex', *S.C.M.* XXI, 1947, 130–1
   'Pumpkin Pie and Other Good Things at the Harvest Feast', *W.S.G.* 1 September 1966
   'St Clement's Day', *S.C.M.* XXI, 1947, 400–2
   'Sussex Sprites and Goblins', *S.C.M.* XVII, 1943, 96–7
   'Sussex Tipteerers with a Traditional Christmas Play', *W.S.G.* 7 Dec. 1967
   'A Tale of Sussex Honey', *S.C.M.* XXIII, 1949, 154–6
   'When Stir-up Sunday Started the Christmas Preparations', *W.S.G.* 18 November 1965
E. C. CAWTE, A. HELM, N. PEACOCK, *English Ritual Drama*, 1967
A. S. COOKE, *Off the Beaten Track in Sussex*, 1911
E. COOMBER, 'Some Sussex Customs', *S.C.M.* I, 1926/7, 117
M. COOPER, 'History of the Villages : Slaugham', *S.C.M.* XXII, 1948, 354–8
B. COPPER, *A Song for Every Season*, 1971
J. C. EGERTON, *Sussex Folk and Sussex Ways*, 1884
J. P. EMSLIE, 'Collecteanea', *Folklore* XXVI, 1915, 162–7
S. EVERSHED, 'The Legend of the Dragon-Slayer of Lyminster', *S.A.C.* XVIII, 1886, 180–3
B. FIRMIN, *An Illustrated Guide to Crowborough*, 1890
T. GEERING, *Our Parish*, 1884

s. GOODMAN, 'New Light on Ebernoe Horn Fair', *S.C.M.* XXIX, 1955, 320–3.

H. D. GORDON, *The History of Harting*, 1877

L. V. GRINSELL, 'Sussex Barrows,' *S.A.C.* LXXV, 1934, 238–9

H. HALL, see W. D. Parish

A. J. C. HARE, *Sussex*, 2nd. ed., 1896

K. HARMER, 'Bewitched', *S.C.M.* XI, 1937, 451–2

G. HASKINS, 'Old Sussex Charms and Superstitions', *S.C.M.* V, 1931, 122

T. W. HORSEFIELD, *The History and Antiquities of Lewes*, 1824

C. G. JOINER, 'The Knucker of Lyminster', *S.C.M.* III, 1929, 845–6

C. LATHAM, 'Some West Sussex Superstitions Lingering in 1868,' *Folk-Lore Record* I, 1878, 1–67

M. A. LOWER, *Chronicles of Pevensey*, 1846
Contributions to Literature, 1854
'Old Speech and Old Manners in Sussex', *S.A.C.* XIII, 1861, 209–36

E. V. LUCAS, *Highways and Byways in Sussex*, 1904

P. H. LULHAM, 'Superstitions in Sussex', *S.C.M.* XIII, 1939, 55–8

M. MARPLES, *White Horses and Other Hill Figures*, 1949

R. MERRIFIELD, 'Magical Games in Sussex', *S.C.M.* XXVI, 1952, 58–63, 122–7
'The Whitsun Ceremonies of Harting Old Club', *S.C.M.* XXVII, 1953, 216–23

A. R. MILTON, 'The Wicked Old Woman', *S.C.M.* XVII, 1943, 47–9

W. D. PARISH, *A Dictionary of Sussex Dialect*, 1875. Second Edition, *Revised, Enlarged and Illustrated*, by Helena Hall, 1957

M. ROBINSON, *A South Down Farm in the Sixties*, 1938

S. E. ROBINSON, 'Tom Reed: A Man and his Lore', *S.C.M.* IX, 1935, 58–60

S.A.C., Sussex Archaeological Collections, 1848 (in progress)

A. SAWYER, 'Sussex Witches and Other Superstitions', *S.C.M.* IX, 1935, 264

F. E. SAWYER, 'Sussex Folklore and Customs Connected with the Seasons', *S.A.C.* XXXIII, 1883, 237–60

F. E. SAWYER, *Sussex Place-Rhymes and Local Proverbs*, 1884

S.C.M. Sussex County Magazine, 1926–1956

S. D. SECRETAN, 'Legend of Rudgwick Church Bell', *S.C.M.* XVII, 1943, 29–30

E. SHOOSMITH, 'The Lundsfords of Whyly', *S.C.M.* III, 1929, 238–42

J. SIMPSON, 'Legends of Chanctonbury Ring', *Folklore* LXXX, 1969, 122–31

S.N.Q., Sussex Notes and Queries, 1926 (in progress)

I. M. STENNING, 'When We Were Children', *S.C.M.* XXVI, 1952, 427–30, 468; XVII, 1953, 72–6

H. S. TOMS, 'Rabbits: A Folklore Note', *S.C.M.* IX, 1935, 698–9

E. M. VENABLES, 'More Memories of Apple Howling', *W.S.G.* 1 Jan. 1967

'WAYFARER', 'Some Sussex Faith Cures', *S.C.M.* II, 1928, 186

B. WILLS, *Shepherds of Sussex*, 1938

S. O. WOOLLEY, 'Rough Music in Sussex', *Folklore* LXIX, 1958, 39
A. R. WRIGHT, *British Calendar Customs*, 1936–40
M. WRIGHT, *Cuckfield: An Old Sussex Town*, 1971
W.S.G., *West Sussex Gazette,* 1853 (in progress)

Note : Old rural buildings and craft displays may be seen at the Weald and Downland Open Air Museum, West Dean, Sussex.

Index of Tale Types

Numbers preceded by AT are from Antti Aarne and Stith Thompson, *The Types of the Folktale* 1961; those with ML are from R. Th. Christiansen, *The Migratory Legends* 1958; those with ML and an asterisk are from K. M. Briggs, *A Dictionary of British Folktales*, 1970–1.

Motif Index

General Index